Creative EMBROIDERY

PRACTICALITIES

Today, creative stitchery is enjoying a worldwide revival.

We are fortunate to have access to an enormous variety of fabrics and threads in hundreds of colors.

Embellishing fabric with stitching has been known since before Roman times and has been not only a popular pastime but a way of creating something which is unique to the maker.

We hope you enjoy the delightful designs for home and family in this book.

KINDS OF EMBROIDERY
There are two basic types of embroidery: *counted thread* (cross-stitch) and *marked* or *freehand* (crewel). Both types are featured in this book. If you are new to embroidery you may find that counted thread embroidery is easier to master than marked embroidery. *Counted thread embroidery* is usually worked from a chart on which each square corresponds to the intersection of a lengthwise and crosswise thread of the fabric; some or all of the squares are filled in with symbols that represent the stitch placement and color. When doing counted thread embroidery, locate the center of the work as indicated in the directions, and count, matching the squares of the chart to the intersections of the thread, and placing a stitch to correspond to each symboled square.

Counted thread embroidery must be worked on evenweave fabric, which has the same number of horizontal and vertical threads in a square inch; this measurement is often called the 'count' of the fabric. For example, 14-count fabric has 14 horizontal and 14 vertical threads per square inch, and can be covered with 14 stitches per linear inch. The higher the count, the finer the fabric and therefore the smaller the embroidery stitch. Often the instructions will tell you to work over two threads. This means to count the intersection of two horizontal and two vertical threads as one (so 22-count fabric worked over two threads is the same as 11-count fabric worked over one thread). You can stitch any charted design on any count evenweave fabric; the higher the count (or the more stitches made per

CONTENTS

Stitch Guide	4
Perfect White Plus	8
Trousseau Treasures	14
A Collar Story	26
Fit for a Princess	32
Beautiful Blooms	40
Embroider a Stencil	50
Charming Cross-stitch	54

inch), the smaller the finished image. (*Needlepoint* is a form of counted thread embroidery but the design is usually painted right on the canvas so all you have to do is cover the painted threads with stitches.) For *marked* or *freehand embroidery* a design is usually drawn or printed on the fabric and then embroidered; if you are a confident embroiderer you can simply work freehand. It is not necessary to use an evenweave fabric for this type of work, but many of the smooth surface evenweave fabrics make lovely backgrounds for it. For the marked embroidery projects in this book, we have included a pull-out sheet with transfer (iron-on) patterns.

CHOOSING FABRIC

It is possible to embroider on almost any kind of fabric, whether of natural or man-made fibers, open weave or close, light hue or dark. Embroidery fabrics are very often named by their manufacturer – Aida, Hardanger, and Lugana are some common types – these names refer to fabrics of different fibers, weaves and thread counts. To Cross-stitch on a non-evenweave fabric, baste a piece of waste canvas (a temporary evenweave fabric) over the design area, work the embroidery, and then pull out the threads of the canvas.

CHOOSING THREAD

There are several kinds of embroidery threads. They come in different thicknesses and sheens, the most common are cotton, although it is possible to find them in silk and rayon as well. The thicker the thread, the bigger the stitch will be. *Six-strand embroidery floss* has a slight sheen, and the plies can be separated to make a finer thread; the directions indicate how many plies should be used for a particular weight of fabric. Some non-divisible types of thread are *matte cotton*, which is fairly thick and has a dull surface, *brilliant embroidery thread*, which has a slight sheen, and *pearl cotton*, which has a high sheen; the last two come in several thicknesses. DMC colors were used in this book; your shop owner will help you match them to another brand.

CHOOSING NEEDLES

For counted thread embroidery use a tapestry needle, which has a large eye and a blunt point that passes easily between the threads of the evenweave fabric. For marked embroidery, use an embroidery needle, which also has a large eye but has a sharp point that is easier to use on finely woven fabrics. (If you are embroidering with knitting yarn, you may want to use a yarn needle, which is bigger than a tapestry needle.)

HOOPS AND FRAMES

To keep the surface of your fabric taut while you work, place it in an embroidery hoop (two adjustable rings that clamp together over the fabric) or tack it to a frame (you can buy a scroll-type frame just for embroidery, or make a frame from artist's stretchers). Never leave work in a hoop when you are not stitching, as it can distort the fabric.

Above: An embroidered jewellery cushion (see page 57)
Left: Three embroidered collars (see pages 26-27)
Right: Embroidering the chintz cushion (see page 43)

Craft Editor: Tonia Todman
Managing Editor: Judy Poulos
Editorial Coordinator: Margaret Kelly
Craft Assistants: Martina Oprey; Rosa Alonso; Tina Murphy; Yvonne Deacon; Jocelyn Mitchell; Paula McPhaill
Production Manager: Nadia Sbisa
Layout: Lulu Dougherty
Finished Art: Stephen Joseph
Cover Design: Christie & Eckermann
Illustrations: Lesley Griffith
Photography: Andrew Elton
Publisher: Philippa Sandall

© J.B. Fairfax Press Pty Ltd 1991
This book is copyright. No part may be reproduced by any process without the written permission of the publisher.

ISBN 0 937769 86 X

STITCH GUIDE

BLANKET STITCH

Useful for decorative edging, this stitch can be worked over an edge or inside the design area. Working from left to right, bring the needle to the right side at A, insert it again at B, bring it to the right side again at C (Fig. 1). Continue, keeping the thread under the needle and the stitches even (Fig. 2).

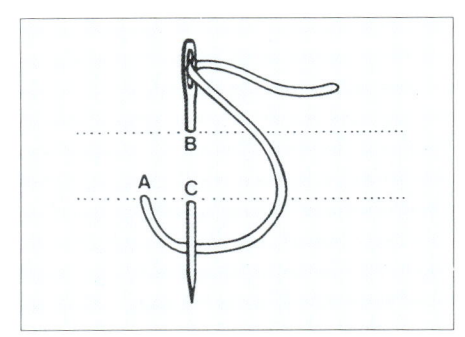

Fig. 1

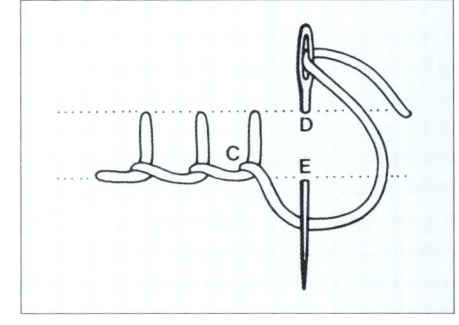

Fig. 2

BULLION STITCH

These are long, thread-wrapped bars, used to add dimension to embroidery. To make a Bullion stitch, bring the needle to the right side at A, insert it at B, bring it to the right side again at A (Fig. 1). Do not pull it through. The distance from A to B equals the length of the finished stitch. Wrap the thread around the needle, covering the length from A to B (Fig. 2). Pull the needle through, easing the wrapped thread onto the fabric. Reinsert at B (Fig. 3).

Pretty rose motifs can be made from an arrangement of Bullion stitches. Place the darkest hue at the centre and the lightest at the edge. Begin at the centre and arrange the stitches in concentric circles, with each stitch at a slight angle to the previous one. Refer to page 22 for some examples.

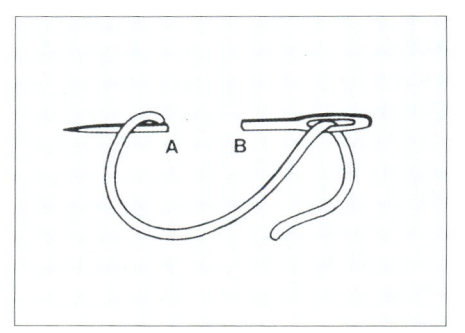

Fig. 1

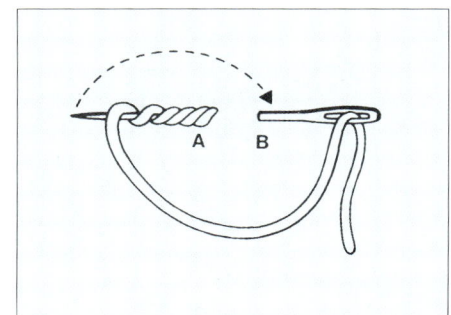

Fig. 2

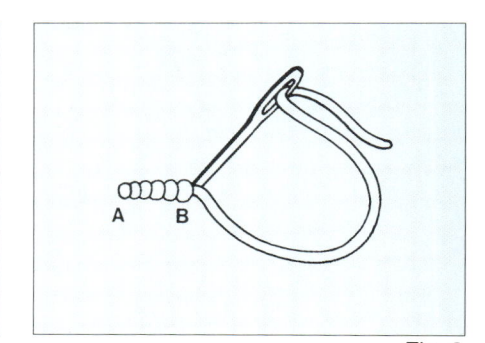

Fig. 3

RAISED BUTTONHOLE STITCH

Buttonhole stitch is worked like Blanket stitch but with the stitches very close together. Outlining the area in small running stitches will give a raised appearance (Fig. 1 and Fig. 2).

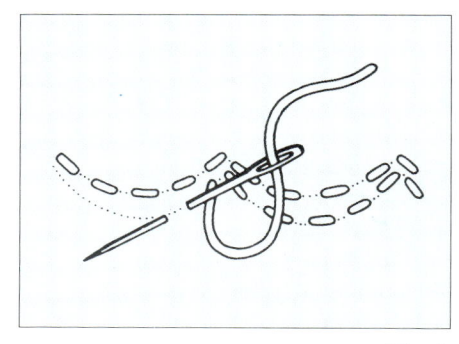

Fig. 1

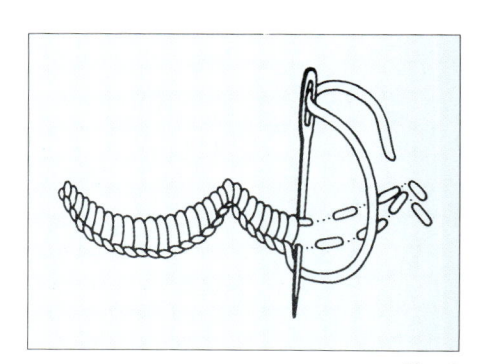

Fig. 2

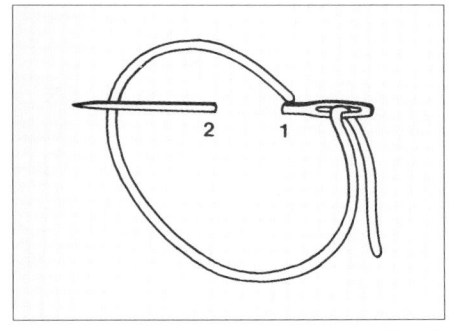

Fig. 1

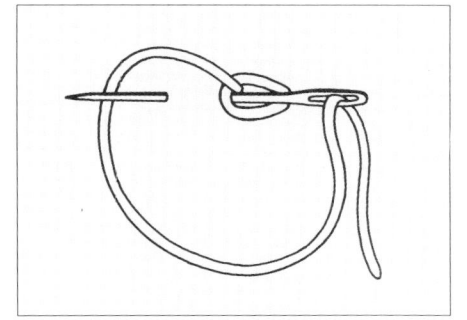

Fig. 2

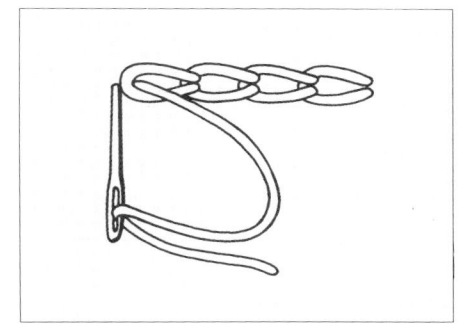

Fig. 3

CHAIN STITCH

Chain stitch is a very versatile embroidery stitch. It can be used in single rows to work a line, to outline or, with rows worked closely together, it can even fill in an area with a block of colour. Work Chain stitch as shown in Fig. 1 and Fig. 2. When the row is complete take a small stitch over the last loop of the chain to secure it as shown in Fig. 3.

CLOSE HERRINGBONE STITCH

This stitch is often used in shadow work embroidery. Always insert the needle from right to left *and* work from left to right. Working on the wrong side of the work, take a stitch at the lower left outline then take a stitch at the upper outline, bringing the needle out on the wrong side and to the left of the thread. Take a stitch back to the lower outline, bringing the needle out on the wrong side as shown in Fig. 1. Continue to work in this way, crisscrossing from left to right filling in the space required.

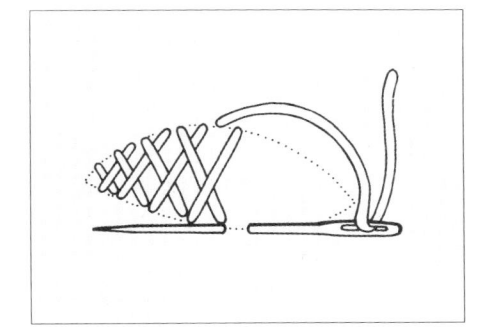

Fig. 1

CROSS-STITCH

Cross-stitch is the most popular embroidery stitch for almost any type of fabric, especially even-weave fabrics whose threads help you place the stitches. Cross-stitch is usually worked in rows of adjacent stitches. One arm of the cross is worked all across the row with the stitches all slanting in the same direction (Fig. 1), then the other arm is worked coming back the other way (Fig. 2). When you work individual Cross-stitches make sure the top arms all slant in the same direction.

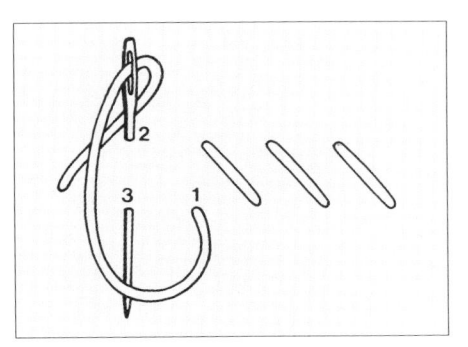

Fig. 1

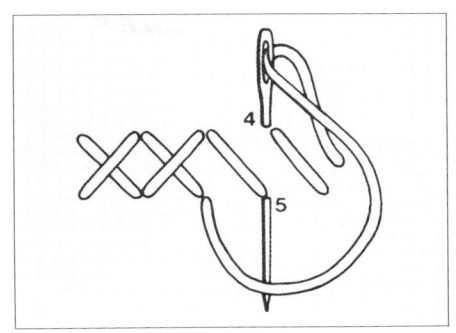

Fig. 2

5

EYELET STITCH

Outline the eyelet area with tiny running stitches. Snip the center (Fig. 1) and trim the threads. Overcast the circle, stitching closely over the raw edge and the running stitches (Fig. 2). You can also use Buttonhole stitches to bind an eyelet (place the bars of the stitches toward the center).

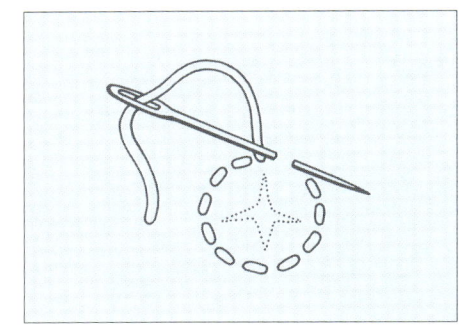

Fig. 1

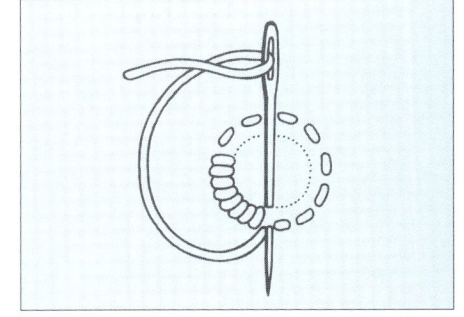

Fig. 2

FRENCH KNOTS

Ideal for flower centers. Begin by bringing the needle to the right side at A; pull the thread through and wrap twice around the needle (Fig. 1). Gently pull the needle through the wrapped thread (Fig. 2) and insert it again close to A. Bring it up again where you want the next French knot.

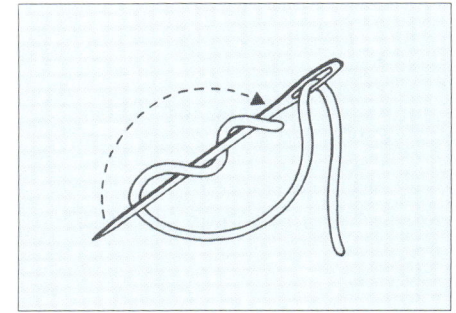

Fig. 1

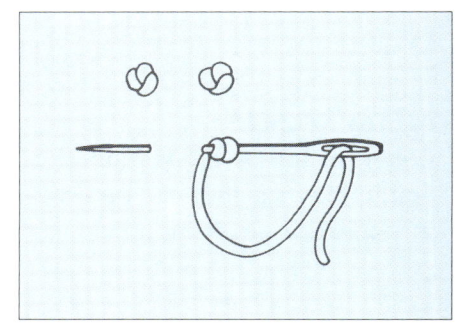

Fig. 2

HEMSTITCH

Draw out the required number of fabric threads. Begin on the wrong side with small backstitches. Working on the right side, pass the needle from right to left under the required number of threads (Fig. 1). Take a small vertical stitch to the right of the thread bundle into the fabric. (Fig. 2).

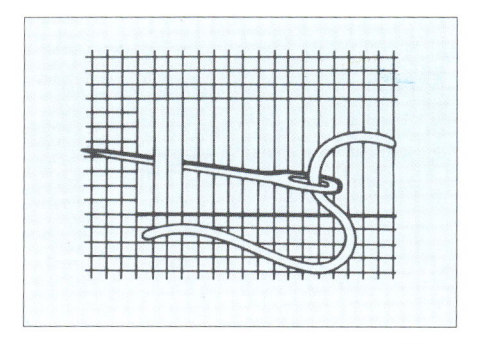

Fig. 1

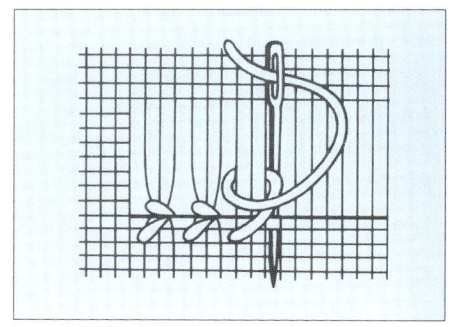

Fig. 2

LAZY DAISY STITCH

Each loop of a Lazy Daisy stitch is made exactly like the last chain of a row of Chain stitches. One loop gives the impression of a flower petal, and 5 or 6 are usually worked into a circle to look like a flower, as the name implies (see Fig. 1, Fig. 2).

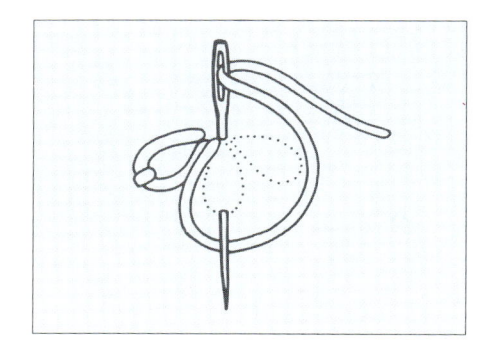

Fig. 1

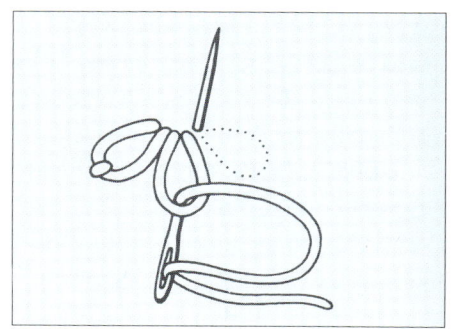

Fig. 2

LONG AND SHORT STITCH

Often used to fill in areas with color. Make adjacent stitches of alternating long and short lengths; in the next row, reverse the alternation (Fig 1). With practice, you can shade the colors by stitching one row in one color and the next in a slightly lighter or darker shade, blending them smoothly.

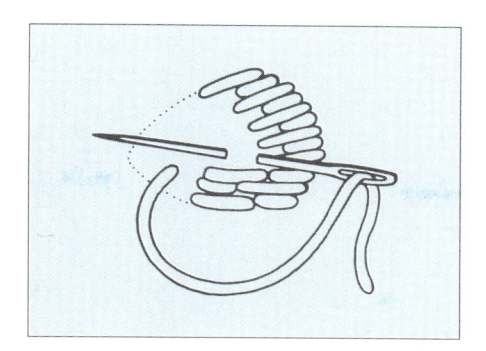

Fig. 1

SATIN STITCH

Use small running stitches to outline the motif. Bring the needle to the right side just outside the motif and insert it again just outside the opposite edge. Repeat, working very closely spaced stitches over the motif, covering the outlining stitches (Fig. 1)

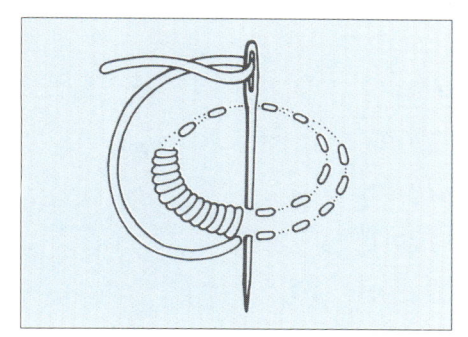

Fig. 1

RAISED SATIN STITCH

Used to give a slightly padded look. Using small running stitches, outline and fill in the area (Fig. 1). Bring the needle to the right side just outside one end of the outlined motif, and working from top to bottom or left to right, work very closely spaced stitches, as for Satin stitch (Fig. 2).

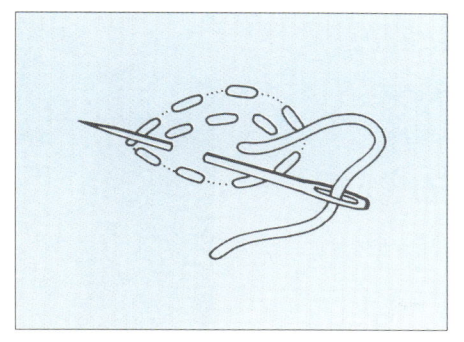

Fig. 1 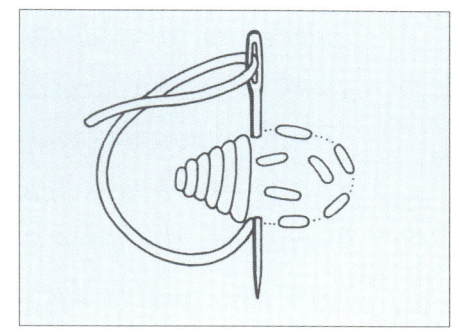   *Fig. 2*

STEM OR OUTLINE STITCH

Used to work the stems on floral motifs. Always insert the needle from right to left *and* work from left to right. Bring the needle to the right side at A, insert at B, bring it up again at C (Fig. 1); then insert it at D, and bring up again at B (Fig. 2). Always keep the thread on the same side of the needle.

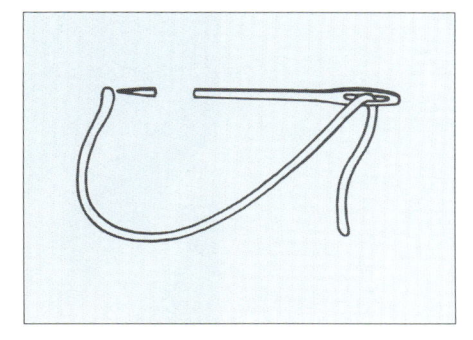

Fig. 1 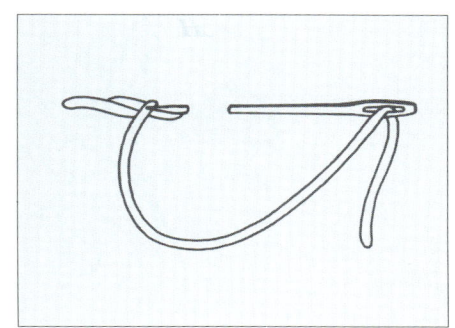   *Fig. 2*

Perfect White Plus

The color of innocence and purity: white is the perfect choice for elegant linen and exquisite underwear. The delightful floral motif we have chosen makes this charming embroidered tablecloth and matching napkins very special. Sheer cotton organdy is perfect for the delicate shadow work while the clear outlines of neatly mitered corners add a classic edge to this heirloom for tomorrow. The same techniques are also used to decorate the delicate camisole and pants.

9

TABLECLOTH AND NAPKINS

Naturally, you can choose any size you wish for your tablecloth, but in practical terms the size will be limited by the width of the fabric. If you must join lengths of fabric to achieve the width you desire, then take care to place the seams at the table edge and not down the center of the cloth.

MATERIALS

a square of cotton organdy, the size of your choice
18" squares of organdy for each napkin
sewing thread
6- strand embroidery floss in the following DMC colors:
  986 (dark green) and white
embroidery needle

METHOD

See the Pull Out Transfer Sheet at the back of the book for the floral motif transfer.
The same basic method is used to make the tablecloth and the napkins.

1 *To prepare your square:* Straighten all the edges of your square of organdy and cut away the selvages. Make sure that the edges follow the grain of the fabric and are not on the bias. Press in 1/2" hems all around the edges. Press in the true hemline $1^{1}/2$" away from the pressed edge.

2 *To miter the corner:* Fold the corner to the right side as shown in Fig. 1, making sure the pressed lines are aligned. Press. Repeat this for each corner. Open out the corners and fold the whole square of fabric in half diagonally, with right sides together and pressed edges even. Stitch along the pressed line as shown in Fig. 2. Trim the fabric at the point and press the seam open as shown in Fig. 3. Turn the corner to the right side. Repeat this for all four corners. Press the corners and hems carefully. Stitch hems into place.

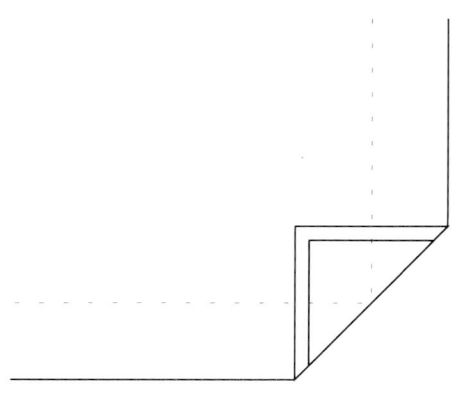

Fig. 1

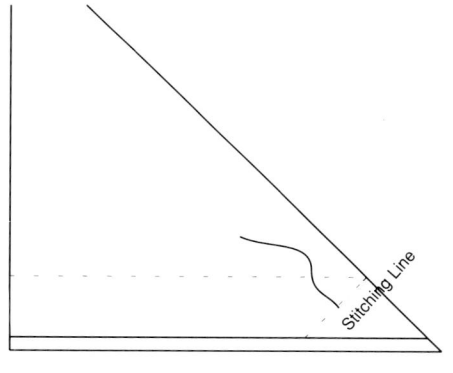

Fig. 2

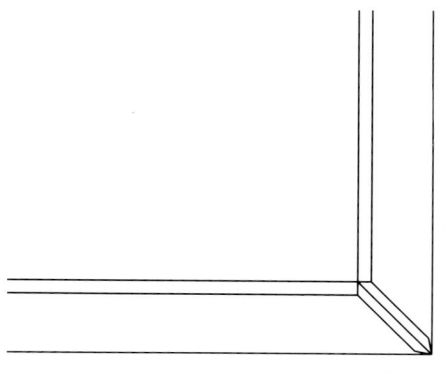

Fig. 3

STITCHES USED

Close Herringbone stitch for the shadow work leaves; Satin stitch for the flowers; Stem stitch for the stems

3 *For the embroidery:* Locate the transfer for the floral motif on the Transfer Sheet. Press the transfer designs into place on the tablecloth, following the directions on the Transfer Sheet. Embroider the leaves, stems and flowers in shadow work, using two strands of embroidery thread and following our Stitch Guide and illustrations at the front of the book. Press the tablecloth and napkins carefully.

Above: A close-up view of the wrong side of the shadow work
Left: Delicate shadow work lilies of the valley decorate this organdy tablecloth and matching napkins

11

CAMISOLE AND PANTS

Delicate underwear is the perfect foil for shadow work embroidery but keep it simple. These bows are the perfect choice.

Note that the camisole and pants are bias-cut.

MATERIALS
1 3/4 yds of 45" wide cotton voile
5 yds of double-edged lace for trimming
tracing paper
pencil
sewing thread
6-strand embroidery floss in DMC 798 (mid-blue) or the color of your choice
embroidery needle
elastic

METHOD
See the Pull Out Pattern Sheet at the back of the book for the pattern. See the Pull Out Transfer Sheet at the back of the book for the embroidery motif.

Pattern Outline
3/8" seams allowed all around each pattern piece.

1 *For cutting out:* Trace the pattern pieces from the pattern sheet. Cut out the pattern pieces from your fabric as directed on the Pattern Sheet, noting they are cut on the bias of the fabric.

2 *For the embroidery:* Press the transfer designs into place on the Camisole and Pants following the directions on the Transfer Sheet. Embroider the bows in shadow work, following the directions for Close Herringbone stitch in the Stitch Guide at the front of the book. Take care not to distort the fabric while you are embroidering – a frame will help you with this.

3 *For the sewing:* Make all seams French seams or normal seams, trimming the seam allowances to 1/4", then neatening them with zigzag stitching or overlocking. Place the front and back camisole pieces together with raw edges even. Stitch the side seams. Place the front and back pants pieces together at the inside legs with raw edges even. Stitch the inside leg seams. Prepare and stitch the crotch seam in the same way, stitching from the front waist through the crotch to the back waist. Sew the side seams.

4 *For the elastic:* Turn 1/4" at the waist edge to the wrong side to neaten, then turn again 5/8". Stitch all around to form a casing for the elastic, leaving a gap for inserting elastic. Insert the elastic, try on the pants and adjust the elastic for comfort. Overlap the ends and stitch together. Close the gap in the casing by hand.

5 *For the lace:* Attach lace to the camisole's upper and lower edges, and the leg edges of the pants in the following way: position the lace so that approximately 7/8 of the lace sits on the fabric and 1/8 is over the edge. Where necessary fold the lace into miters or angles that will allow it to follow the fabric shape. Set your sewing machine stitch controls to a narrow zigzag stitch that is almost a Satin stitch. Stitch around the pattern of the lace close to the inner edge. Trim away the voile from underneath the lace and the excess lace inside the stitching on the right side. Topstitch

STITCHES USED
Close Herringbone stitch for the shadow work bows

any angles or miters that need to be secured, using a narrow zigzag stitch.

6 *For the straps:* Measure the length for your shoulder straps and cut two pieces of bias fabric this length plus $1\frac{1}{4}$" x $\frac{3}{4}$". Fold the strips in half lengthwise with right sides together. Stitch twice for strength along the long side. Turn the straps right side out. Pin the straps in place on the front and back of the camisole so that the raw ends of the straps are tucked underneath, out of sight. Try on the camisole to adjust the strap length then handsew the ends into place.

Top left: The shadow work bow seen from the right side
Above left: The same bow viewed from the wrong side
Above: The camisole and pants with lace trim and embroidered bows

To turn spaghetti straps if you don't own a gadget made specially for the purpose, thread a large darning needle with a strong, double thread. Stitch securely at one end of the strap, then pass the needle down the length and out the other end. Pulling gently on the double thread, turn the strap to the right side.

14

Trousseau Treasures

Not so long ago, young girls began preparing and putting aside beautiful bed linen and towels for a 'hope chest' or 'glory box'. These days, although the pace of life seems to have overtaken this charming old tradition, hand-embroidered treasures like these still delight the bride-to-be.

Clockwise from the left: The voile nightgown; cushion, p. 46; embroidered sheets and pillowcases; Bullion stitch rose embroidered towels and cross stitch embroidered towels

A Voile Nightgown

A soft, pure cotton, voile nightgown that's been embroidered with loving care would be a delightful addition to any trousseau. This simple style has been trimmed with lace and shadow work bows, and scattered with Bullion stitch roses.

STITCHES USED
Close Herringbone stitch for the bow; French Knots on the bow; Bullion stitch for the roses and leaves; Stem stitch for the stems

MATERIALS
3 yds of 45" wide cotton voile
2 3/4 yds of good quality bias binding (either cotton or satin)
2 3/4 yds of fine cotton cording for piping
2 3/4 yds of 1/2" wide white satin ribbon for facing
2 1/4 yds of ribbon in the same color as the shadow embroidery for the sash
4 1/3 yds of 3" wide lace for the bodice and hem trim
6-strand embroidery floss in the colors of your choice or DMC colors 793 (dark blue), 794 (light blue), 988 (green) and white
matching sewing thread
embroidery needle

METHOD
See the Pull Out Transfer Sheet at the back of the book for the bow motif. See the Pull Out Pattern Sheet at the back of the book for the nightgown pattern.

Pattern Outline
3/8" seams allowed all around each pattern piece.

1 *For cutting out:* Cut out the nightgown front and back pattern pieces as directed on the Pattern Sheet. Cut approximately 2 1/4 yds of 1 1/4" wide bias strips from the fabric for shoulder straps.

2 *For the embroidery:* Iron the bow motif onto the center front of the nightgown, following the directions on the Transfer Sheet. Embroider the motif using two strands of embroidery thread in Close Herringbone stitch, French knots and the Bullion stitch roses as instructed in the Stitch Guide at the front of the book. Embroider the roses around the bow.

3 *For the lace and piping:* Gather the lace just enough to cause it to stand away from the fabric when applied. Press open the bias binding and then fold in half, wrong sides together. Using the zipper foot of your sewing machine, stitch the piping cord into the fold of the bias binding.

4 *For the sewing:* Join the front to the back nightgown at the side seams using narrow French seams or a normal seam with the allowance stitched together 1/4" from the seam, trimmed back close to the stitching and overcast. Be sure to leave one side seam open for up to 12" from hem for a split.

5 *For the lace:* With the right sides together and raw edges matching, baste the lace around the hem and side split. Make small pleats if necessary to ease the lace around the corners and curves. Gradually ease the lace away to nothing at the top of the split so it looks as if it disappears into the top of the split. Using a fine zigzag stitch and sewing 1/4" in from the edge, stitch the lace around the hem and side split. Trim away the seam allowances close to the stitching. With the wrong side of the lace facing the right side of the gown and starting at a side seam, baste the lace around the upper bodice in the same way.

6 *For the piping:* Pin and baste the piping on top of the lace at the

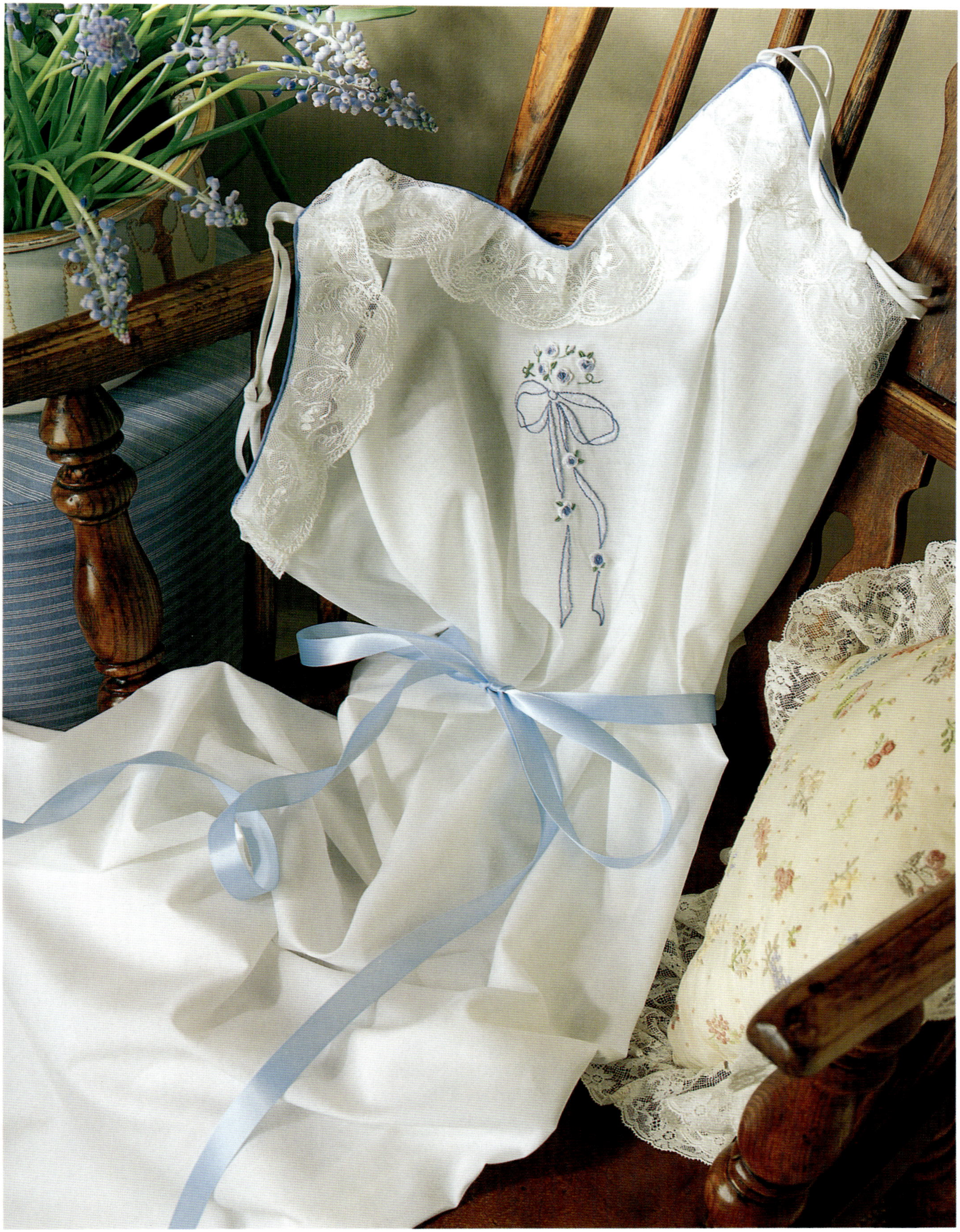

upper bodice, with raw edges matching. Tuck the raw end of the piping under at the overlap. Stitch the piping in place using the zipper foot and with the sewing machine needle nearer to the cord or on top of the previous piping stitching. Clip seam allowances where necessary for ease. Press the seam to the inside.

Above: The top of the nightgown showing the delicate lace, piping and spaghetti shoulder straps
Left: A shadow work embroidered bow and Bullion stitch roses trim the lovely nightgown

7 *For the shoulder straps:* Fold the bias strips of fabric in half lengthwise with right sides together and raw edges even. Stitch down the long side, trim the seam and turn the straps to the right side. Try on the nightgown to adjust the length of the shoulder straps. Using two lengths of strap for each shoulder, fold each length in half and loop one through the other in the middle, so that the loop sits on the shoulder and the raw ends are at the front and the back. Handsew the raw ends in place. On the inside, handsew the 1/2" wide ribbon over the seam allowance with the top edge of the ribbon on the piping stitching, pleating the ribbon where necessary around the angles and covering the ends of the shoulder straps. Make two thread loops on the side seams at waist level, or just above, to hold the sash.

To turn rouleau straps if you don't own a gadget made specially for the purpose, thread a large darning needle with a strong, double thread. Stitch securely at one end of the rouleau, then pass the needle down through the length and out the other end. Pulling gently on the double thread, turn the rouleau to the right side.

EMBROIDERED TOWELS

You can buy towels with the evenweave fabric panel already included and ready to be Cross-stitched. If you can't buy them where you shop, you can find an evenweave band with bound edges at craft shops. Cross-stitch it, then sew onto the towel. Either way, these charming confections of ribbons, roses, rabbits and hearts should grace any bathroom.

MATERIALS
a suitable towel with or without an evenweave band
14-threads-to-the-inch evenweave band to embroider
6-strand embroidery floss in colors of your choice. We used DMC colors 3354, 800 and white
a suitable needle

METHOD
See the Pull Out Pattern Sheet at the back of the book for the embroidery charts.

1. *For the Cross-stitch towel:* Find the center of the band to be embroidered by folding or measuring lengthwise and crosswise. Sew lines of loose running stitch along the folds. The intersection of these lines marks the center point which corresponds with the center of the chart. To find the center of the chart, join the arrows at each side with a ruler. The point of intersection is the center.

2. Each symbol on the chart represents one Cross-stitch and the different symbols indicate the colors to be used in the embroidery. Cross-stitch the motifs following the Stitch Guide at the front of the book, counting the threads and using the chart as a guide. Use two strands of floss. Do not pull the threads too tightly and make sure you begin and end by running the needle through the back of a few stitches to secure the ends.

3. If you are using an evenweave band, turn under the raw ends and machine stitch the band in place across the towel.

For the Bullion stitch rose towels: Stitch sprays of Bullion stitch roses, following the Stitch Guide at the front of the book. Trim with bands of lace and ribbon or satin ribbon-trimmed grosgrain as shown. Tie the ribbon into a bow and secure with small stitches.

Stitch the Bullion stitch rose towels in DMC colors: cream (746); yellow (727 and 726); pink (963, 962 and 961); peach (754, 353 and 352) and green (368 and 320).

STITCHES USED
Cross-stitch for the rabbits and hearts; Bullion stitch roses and leaves

19

EMBROIDERED BED LINEN

There is nothing like the feeling of slipping between crisp cotton sheets. These ones have an heirloom quality in their pretty embroidery. Trim the bed linen with colours that accent your bedroom scheme and add some beautiful cotton lace for that final touch.

MATERIALS

purchased cotton pillowcases and one flat cotton sheet
6-strand embroidery floss in colors of your choice. We used DMC colors 783, 445, 307 and 444
5" wide cotton single-edged lace
1/2" wide satin ribbon
embroidery needle

METHOD

See the Pull Out Transfer Sheet at the back of the book for the embroidery designs.

PILLOWCASE

1 *For the ribbon and lace:* Pin the lace around the pillowcase opening so that the lacy edge just overhangs the pillowcase opening, beginning and ending at a side seam. Open the pillowcase seam at that point for 5" to allow the raw ends of the lace to extend through to the wrong side. Stitch the lace in place. Pin and stitch the ribbon in place so that it covers the raw edge of the lace; extend it into the seam as well. Stitch the seam closed.

2 *For the design:* Find and mark the center of the lace on top of the pillowcase by measuring or folding it in half lengthwise and crosswise. Locate the monogram and floral design on the Transfer Sheet and iron the transfers onto the center of the lace as instructed on the Transfer Sheet.

3 *For the embroidery:* Embroider the motifs using two strands of thread and following the Stitch Guide at the front of the book. Press.

STITCHES USED

Raised Satin stitch for the monograms, flowers and leaves; Eyelet stitch for flower centres; Stem stitch for the stems

SHEETS

Follow steps 1, 2 and 3 in the Method, omitting the instructions relating to the opening of the side seam of the pillowcase.

21

THE ROSE GARDEN

Bullion stitch roses are a charming embroidery motif for delicate lingerie, bath towels, sleepwear or bed linen. The arrangement of the roses need only be limited by your imagination. Here are a few ideas to inspire you. Note that you can combine Bullion stitch roses with many other embroidery stitches, such as the French knots indicated here by filled circles, to give the effect you are looking for. On the next page you will see how designs like these have been applied in actual embroidery.

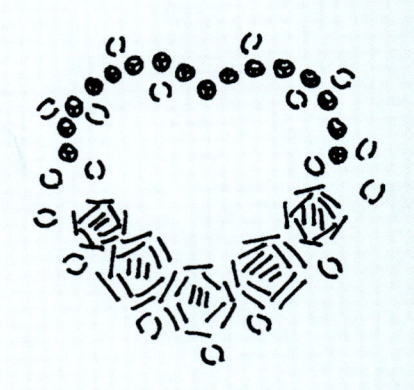

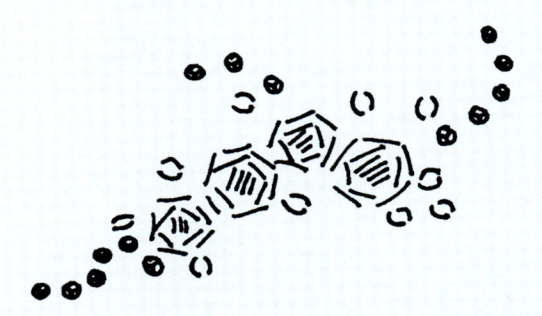

23

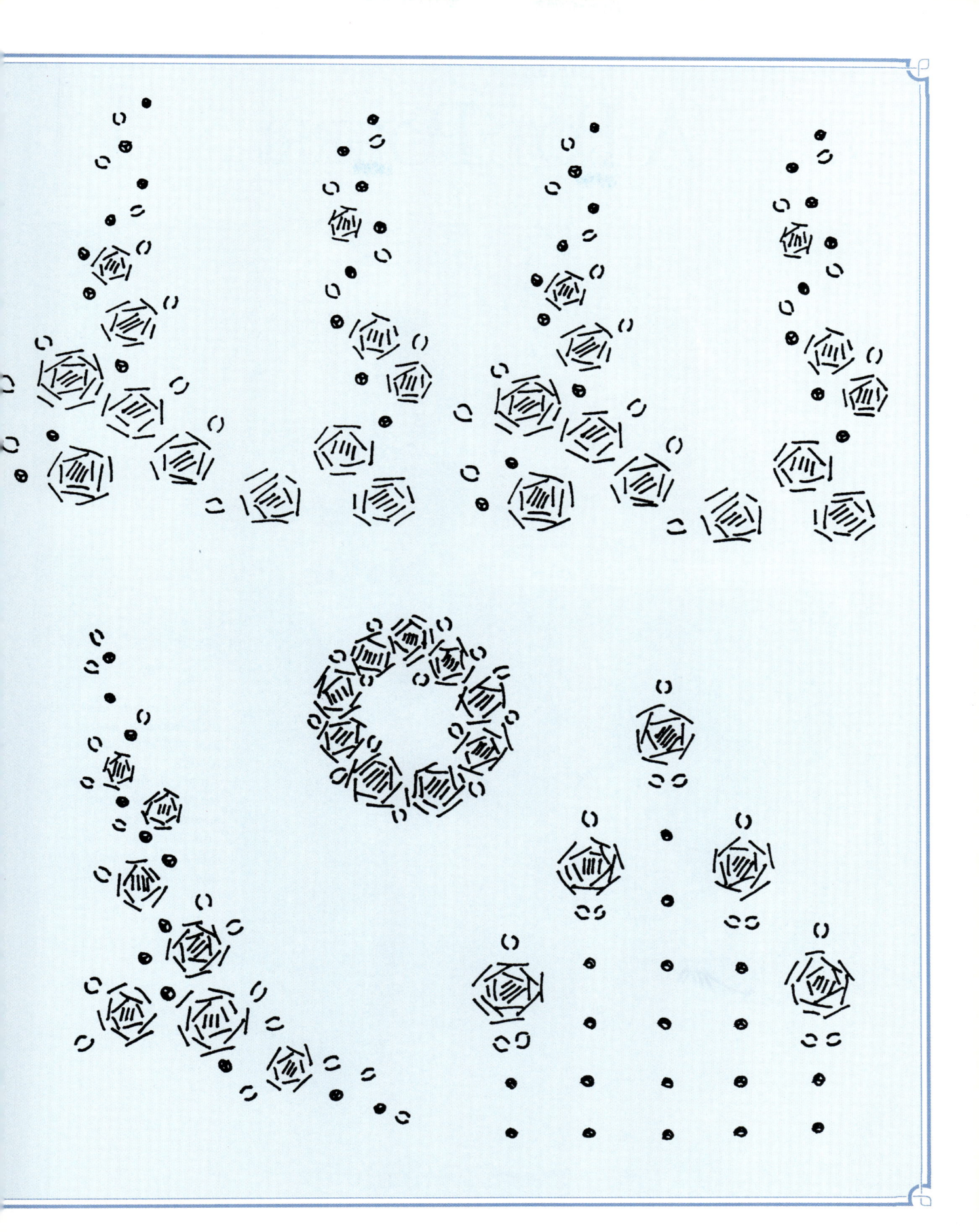

A Pot Pourri

Top left: A purchased face cloth takes on a special look with embroidered roses
Above: Trim a net drape for baby's bassinet with a sprinkle of roses
Left: This delicate voile dress is charming with its embroidered yoke and hem

Right: Pretty as well as practical, this bathrobe is a touch of luxury
Below right: For the bride and groom on their wedding day, embroider a cover for their wedding photo album
Below: Dainty Bullion stitch roses are the perfect finishing touch for these lingerie bags

25

A Collar Story

A crisp, white collar can add the finishing touch to any young lady's special outfit. Even better if the collar is embroidered or personally monogrammed with her initials. Make the collar removable for washing, then she won't have to keep it for 'best' but can wear it anytime at all.

27

ORGANDY COLLAR

Scallops of traditional organdie, delicately embroidered, make this collar ideal for a seven-year-old girl.

MATERIALS
2/3 yd of 36" wide cotton organdy
tracing paper
pencil
6-strand embroidery floss in your choice of colors
sewing thread
embroidery needle
button

METHOD
See the Pull Out Pattern Sheet at the back of the book for the collar pattern. See the Pull Out Transfer Sheet at the back of the book for the embroidery designs.

Pattern Outline
3/8" seam allowance is included on each pattern piece, unless otherwise indicated.

1 *For cutting out:* Trace the complete collar pattern from the Pattern Sheet, using the tracing paper and pencil. Transfer any symbols and markings. Using this as your pattern, cut out two fronts and four backs from organdy (one front and two backs will be the facing). Trace the scalloped border pattern from the complete collar pattern on the Pattern Sheet. Using this as your guide, cut out a scalloped border strip for each front and both backs (two front borders and four back borders in total). Cut a strip of fabric 15 1/4" x 2 1/2" for the neckband.

2 *For the sewing:* Pin the scalloped border strips to the outer edges of the wrong side of each collar piece. Baste all around and from here on treat these as a single piece. Join the collar front to the collar backs at the shoulders. Repeat this for the facing. Place the collar and facing together so that raw edges are even. Stitch all around, leaving the neck edge open. Trim the fabric at the corners and clip the seams where necessary. Turn the collar right side out, pushing out the fabric very carefully around the scalloped edges. Baste the neckband around the collar neckline, with right sides together and raw edges even. Stitch around the neckline. Fold the neckband in to the wrong side and press under 1/4" on remaining raw edge of neckband. Fold neckband in half lengthwise with right sides together. Stitch across the short ends 1/2" beyond the edges of the scallops. Turn the band right side out, and hand sew the inner folded edge to the neckline stitching. Stitch carefully along the inner edge of the border through all thicknesses, joining the collar and the facing. Make a buttonhole on the neckband at the right edge. Sew on the button to correspond with the buttonhole.

3 *For the embroidery:* Using two strands of floss, embroider the Bullion stitch roses as shown.

STITCHES USED
Bullion stitch for the roses and leaves; Stem stitch for the stems

Circular Linen Collar

MATERIALS
1/2 yd of 36" wide handkerchief linen
tracing paper
pencil
6-strand embroidery floss in the colors of your choice. We have used DMC colors 368; 3347; 603; 605; 796; 800; 3078; 761; 211; 818
4 1/4 yds narrow cotton lace edging
one small flat button
sewing thread
embroidery needle

METHOD
See the Pull Out Transfer Sheet at the back of the book for the collar patterns and embroidery designs.
Pattern Outline
3/8" seams allowed all around each pattern piece.

1. *For cutting out:* Cut out the pattern piece from the Transfer Sheet and iron the entire transfer onto a single layer of fabric. Cut out the collar shape. Note that the cutting line is the transfer line at the edge of the collar and that 3/8" seam allowances have been included. Using the transfer paper as your pattern, cut out another collar shape. Cut two 14" x 1 1/4" bias strips of linen for the neckbands which extend into the ties.

2. *For the embroidery:* Embroider the flowers on the collar front using two strands of embroidery floss, following the Stitch Guide in the front of the book.

3. *For the neckbands:* Fold the strip of fabric for the neckbands in half lengthwise with right sides together. Stitch across both short ends and down the raw long edge of each neckband, leaving a 7" gap in the stitching at one end. Turn the ties to the right side and press carefully. Baste the 7" raw edges of the ties to the neckline of the embroidered collar, starting 3/8" from the back opening, and so that the neckbands meet at the center front.

4. *To finish off:* Stitch the lace around the embroidered collar, so that the straight edge of the lace extends into the seam allowance and the decorative edge points toward the neck edge. Pin and baste the remaining plain collar piece over the embroidered collar. Stitch around all the edges, following the stitching line for the lace and the neckbands, and leaving an opening in one center back edge for turning. Trim the corners and clip into the curved seams for ease. Turn the collar right side out, hand sew the opening closed and press it carefully. Make a buttonhole on the right center back at the neck edge. Sew a button on the left side to correspond with the buttonhole. Make a bow with the ties at the center front.

Fine linen is the perfect choice for a delicate collar, monogrammed and embroidered, for a five-year-old little miss.

STITCHES USED
Raised Satin stitch for the flowers, leaves and bow centers; Eyelet stitch for the flower centers; Stem stitch for the stems and outline; Long and Short stitch for the bows

Tie-on Baby's Collar

This sweet tie-on collar for babies will stay in place no matter how much they wriggle or how many cuddles they get.

STITCHES USED
Raised Satin stitch for the monogram, flowers and leaves; Eyelet stitch for the flowers centres; Stem stitch for the stems and outlining; Long and Short stitch for the bows; Blanket stitch for the edging

MATERIALS
1/2 yd of 36" wide handkerchief linen
tracing paper; pencil
1 yd of 3/8" wide satin ribbon for side ties (or you can make linen ties from scraps)
3 small, flat buttons
6-strand embroidery floss in colors of your choice. We have used DMC colors 827; 3716; 962; 772; 211; 746; 445; 471
sewing thread
embroidery needle

METHOD
See the Pull Out Pattern Sheet at the back of the book for the collar pattern. See the Pull Out Transfer Sheet at the back of the book for the embroidery motifs.

Pattern Outline
3/8" seams allowed all around each pattern piece.

1 *For cutting out:* Cut out the front and back collar pattern pieces as directed on the Pattern Sheet. Be sure to cut two fronts, four backs and four collar pieces.

2 *For the embroidery:* Locate the monogram you require and the floral motif on the Transfer Sheet. Iron the motifs onto one front collar piece. Embroider the motifs in two strands of embroidery floss following the Stitch Guide at the front of the book. You may like to embroider the motifs using floss in shades that reflect the colors of the dress over which the collar is worn, or you may like to make it quite neutral so that it can be worn with several dresses.

3 *For the sewing:* When you have finished the embroidery, press the fabric pieces carefully, then join the front to the backs at the shoulders. Place the small curved collar pieces together in pairs, with right sides together and raw edges even. Stitch around the larger curved edge. Clip into the curves for ease. Turn the small collars right side out. Press.

4 *To assemble the collars:* Stitch around each small collar and the main collar with small buttonhole stitches in a color used in the flower embroidery, using two strands of floss. Baste the small collars around the neckline of the main embroidered collar. Pin one 8" length of ribbon 3/4" above each lower outer corner (two on the front and one each on the backs) with raw edges matching. Place main collars right sides together. Stitch around the edge, leaving an opening for turning along one center back edge. Take care not to catch the ties as you sew. Trim seams and corners, clipping where necessary for ease. Turn the collar right side out and press. Close the opening by hand.

5 *To finish off:* Make three buttonholes on the right back, placing one at the neckline and the others 2" apart. Sew the buttons on the left back to correspond with the buttonholes.

31

Fit for a Princess

She will certainly look like a princess in her special dress with its traditional smocking and embroidery.

33

Simple Smocking

Smocking began as the first 'elastic' but has become a delightful and creative technique for trimming babies' and children's clothes. Follow these illustrated steps to master the technique and some of the most common smocking stitches.

1 Mark an even grid of dots on wrong side of fabric with a purchased smocking dot transfer. You can also place carbon paper under the fabric and, pinning graph paper on top, press firmly to mark dots.

2 Gathering up dots: Using strong, doubled thread in a contrasting colour, begin at right-hand side and pick up each dot across fabric. Leave threads hanging at ends.

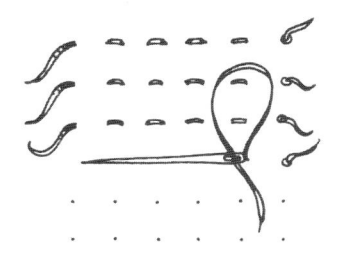

3 Pulling up: Pull up threads to desired width, for example width of yoke. Tie off threads firmly in pairs. Pull up firmly, but not tightly. Secure threads. Begin smocking on right-hand side. Remove gathering threads when smocking is complete.

OUTLINE STITCH: Work stitch with thread above needle as shown and keeping stitches tight.

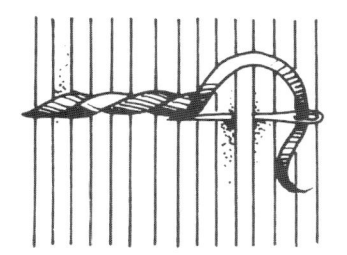

WAVE STITCH: Work stitches firmly although angles make this stitch very elastic. Always work between two rows of gathering stitches, beginning at lower left corner and working up as shown. When ascending, thread lies under needle and below when descending.

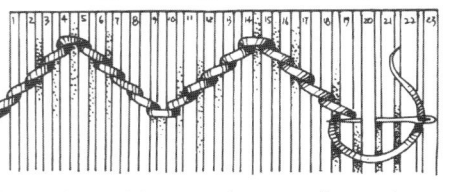

HONEYCOMBING STITCH: One of the oldest smocking stitches, it is very elastic and simple to do. Stagger starting points of stitches, working over two folds.

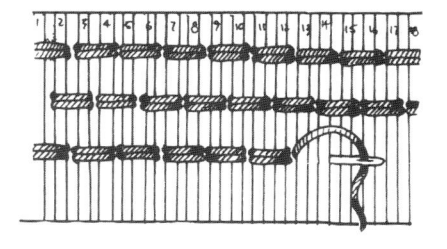

SURFACE HONEYCOMB: This stitch is elastic and very decorative, exposing more thread. It can be built up into panels by mirror reversing the panels.

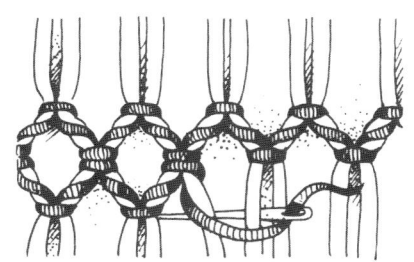

BULLION KNOTS: Are worked as if embroidering, but take care to begin and end stitches on folds as shown.

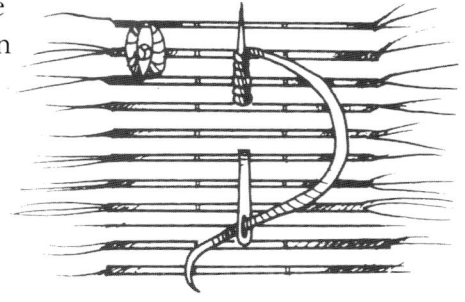

Smocked Dress
For a Five-Year-Old

DETACHABLE COLLAR

See the Pull Out Transfer Sheet at the back of the book for the smocking dots.

1. Using the dress front as your pattern, trace a piece that follows the neckline and shoulder lines. Mark points $3\frac{1}{4}$" from the neckline in an arc from one shoulder to the other. Repeat this for the back. These pieces will form the underlay of the smocked collar that tucks inside the dress neck. Cut one front and two backs of this pattern from the dress fabric, taking care to cut them along straight grainlines. Join the front and backs of the underlay pieces at the shoulders. Neaten the outside edge by hemming, overlocking or zigzag stitching.

2. Cut out the collar, using the pattern in the pattern packet, from the dress fabric and not from the lace as shown on the pattern packet. Smock the collar as instructed in the pattern packet and in 'Simple Smocking' on page 34. Press under $\frac{1}{2}$" on the outer edge of the smocked collar. Stitch.

3. Ease the collar to the size of the neckline and baste it around the neckline of the underlay. Cut a 2" wide bias strip from the fabric. Press it in half lengthwise, right sides together. Place this bias on top of the collar with all raw edges matching. Stitch it in place, joining the underlay, collar and bias strip as you sew.

4. Make a thread loop on the center right back and sew a small button onto the left center back to correspond with the loop. You may like to have small snaps on the inside shoulder of the dress and on the collar underlay to help keep the collar in place.

SLEEVES

See the Pull Out Transfer Sheet at the back of the book for the smocking dots.

1. Find the center of the sleeve pattern by folding it in half and rule a line from the top to the lower edge. Cut through the pattern along this line. Place the pattern pieces onto the fabric, spreading the two halves 6" apart. Iron on a band of smocking dots $1\frac{1}{2}$" deep across the sleeves, $1\frac{1}{2}$" from the lower edge. Smock the sleeves in the same stitches as were used on the collar.

2. Press under $\frac{1}{2}$" on the sleeve ends. Stitch. Stitch the underarm seam. Gather the sleeve cap and sew sleeves into dress armholes. Neaten armhole edges with overlocking or zigzag stitching.

This lovely little dress has two detachable collars – one smocked to match the dress and the other taken from A Collar Story on page 26 embroidered with flowers. We have used Simplicity pattern No. 9579 for the dress. Follow the pattern instructions but take note of our changes to the Collar and Sleeves instructions.

STITCHES USED
Honeycomb stitch and Surface Honeycomb stitch

SMOCKED DRESS FOR A SEVEN-YEAR-OLD

We have added smocking and colored piping to this otherwise simple dress. The detachable organdy collar from 'A Collar Story' is embroidered to reflect the print in the dress fabric and more small Bullion stitch roses have been added to the sleeve cuffs. The smocking is also in colors to match the dress. Start with a purchased pattern for a simple, dirndle-skirted dress.

Select from any of the smocking stitches shown on page 34 to smock the panel in the centre front of the dress. Follow the pattern maker's instructions for making the dress, but note our changes below.

1 *For the smocking on the skirt:*
See the Pull Out Transfer Sheet at the back of the book for the smocking dots.
Divide the skirt front width into eight panels. Transfer the smocking dots to the center six panels of the skirt, leaving one panel clear on either side. Gather up the dots and embroider smocking to the desired depth, using the stitches in our 'Simple Smocking' guide on page 34. Adjust the finished width of the skirt to match the lower edge of the bodice. Read the piping instructions before joining the skirt to the bodice.

2 *For the piping at waist and cuffs:*
In addition to the materials listed on the pattern pack you will need enough bias binding and cotton cording for the waist and both cuffs. Unfold the length of bias binding. Press, then fold it in half catching a length of narrow piping cord in the fold. When the bodice is assembled, baste the piping around the lower edge of the bodice, with the piping on right side of fabric and keeping raw edges even. Attach skirt as instructed. Repeat these steps for the lower edges of the sleeves after gathering but before attaching the cuffs.

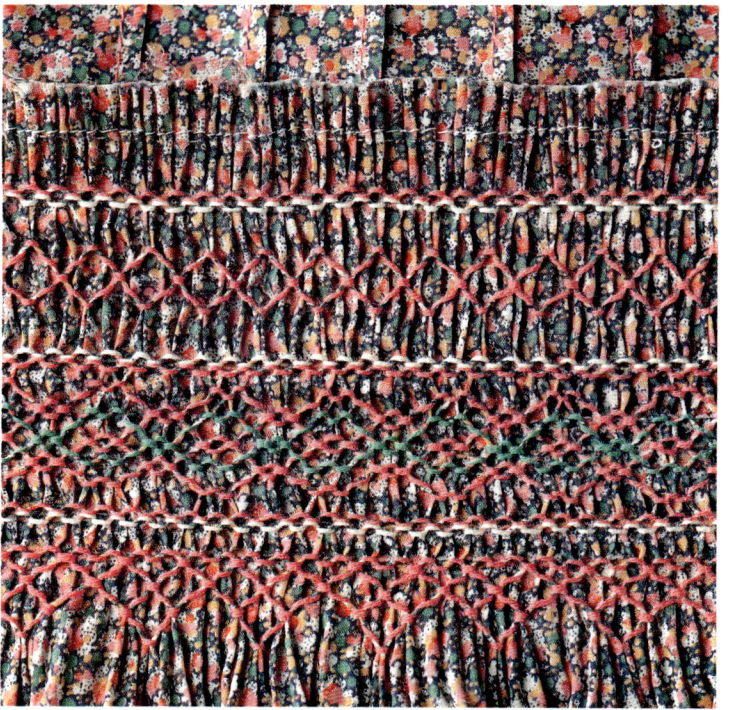

3 *For the Bullion stitch roses:*
Make small Bullion stitch roses using two or three strands of floss at the center of the cuffs, following the instructions in the Stitch Guide at the front of the book. Make as many as you like to form a pleasing pattern.

Left: Close up of the smocking

STITCHES USED
Surface Honeycomb stitch

Smocked Dress For a Baby

SIZE: 6 to 12 months

MATERIALS
1 1/4 yds of 45" wide fabric
three small buttons
1 1/2 yds cotton lace
6-strand embroidery floss for smocking
tracing paper and pencil

METHOD
See the Pull Out Pattern Sheet at the back of the book for the pattern. See the Pull Out Transfer Sheet at the back of the book for the smocking dots.
Pattern Outline
3/8" seams allowed all around each pattern piece.

1 *For cutting out:* Trace the pattern pieces from the Pattern Sheet. Cut out the pattern pieces as instructed.

2 *For the smocking:* Smock the dress front following the instructions in Simple Smocking on page 34. Pull up the smocking to the width of the front yoke.

3 *For the yoke:* Sew front yoke to back yokes at shoulders with right sides together. Press seams open. Sew the front yoke facing to the back yoke facings (extensions of back yoke), with right sides together. Press seams open. Fold yoke facings over yokes so that right sides are together. Stitch around the neck edge. Trim the seam, clip curves. Turn the facing right side out. Press. Pin front yoke to front skirt with right sides together. Stitch, taking care to leave the front yoke facing free.

4 *For the skirt:* Stitch the center back skirt seam up to the facing extensions. Neaten the extension edges. Pin the back yokes to the back skirt as far as the foldline on the back yokes. Fold the back extensions to the inside along the foldlines, forming facings. Stitch through all thicknesses, taking care to leave the back yoke facing free. Press all seams towards yoke. Turn under seam allowance on raw lower edges of yoke facings.

5 *For the sleeves:* Baste together the raw armhole edges of the yokes and from here on treat them as a single layer. Gather the sleeve caps. Sew the sleeves into the armholes, adjusting the gathering to fit. Neaten the armhole edges with overlocking or zigzag stitching. Turn under 1 1/2" at the sleeve ends. Stitch the raw edge down with two rows of stitching to form the casings. Join the ends of the lace and stitch it around the sleeve ends, just under the edge as shown. Thread elastic through the casings, adjust the length and secure the ends.

6 *To finish off:* Sew the side seams from wrist to hem. Turn up the skirt hem. Press. Join the ends of the lace together. Baste the lace around the hem, just under the edge as shown. Stitch, fixing the hem and lace in place as you go. Make buttonholes in back yoke. Sew on buttons.

STITCHES USED
Honeycomb stitch; Surface Honeycomb stitch; Outline stitch; Wave stitch; Bullion stitch

THE SMOCKING STORY

Smocking is a technique of decorating fabric which actually becomes part of the shaping and construction of the garment. As a technique it has been around for hundreds of years and probably long before that. Because of the perishable nature of cotton fabric, there are few examples of very old smocking but we have evidence from the paintings of the fifteenth century that smocked garments were in vogue even then. Originally, clothing was simply cut and with little or no shaping, apart from being caught up in a belt or a girdle. Later, as a more generous use of fabric became the practice, a way had to be found to drape and shape fabric to the body and then to secure that shaping in some way, and smocking was born. Not only did smocking shape the garment but it added some elasticity and a way of adding decoration at the same time.

The earliest reference using the word 'smocking' dates from the fourteenth century. The technique seems to take its name from the smocks which were worn by the wealthy as an undergarment and by the peasants as an outer shirt. Originally the shirts, or smocks, were simple, undecorated garments but became increasingly more ornate. In England by the eighteenth century we were seeing beautiful examples of hand stitching and embroidery that are now recognised as smocking. Shepherds' smocks were worn until relatively recently as the shepherd's lifestyle in the early part of this century was little changed from that of a hundred years before. He would wear his best smock, lovingly decorated by his wife or mother, to the fairs and gatherings. Naturally this inspired considerable competition among the ladies of the village to see who could produce the most beautiful smock. Later on, the smocks became available to buy in the towns but were still highly prized garments, costing a great deal of money and were often passed down from father to son.

Holland or linen drill was the fabric used for smocks at this time. As the name implies, this fabric was imported from the Netherlands. Later a heavy cotton fabric, milled in England, gradually replaced it. The smocking and embroidery, even on the commercially-produced smocks, was often done by individual women working in their own homes – an early cottage industry as well as a craft.

The most popular smock was the round smock which was worn 'all the way round', the front being turned around to the back when it was dirty. When that too was dirty, the smock was washed. A very practical idea! Traditionally, the round smock was smocked in panels on the collar, cuffs and yokes. The embroidery often reflected the trade of the wearer or the area of its origin.

Later, with the advent of the industrial revolution, loose clothing, and the lifestyle it embodied, became less and less acceptable. However, children continued to wear smocks particularly to protect their clothes. Small children and babies wore 'dresses' in fine linen smocked around the neck, yoke and cuffs, and these are still worn today.

Smocking is the only form of embroidery that affects the actual shape of a garment, as the drawing in of the fabric fullness needed for smocking will naturally shape it. Today, smocking is being stitched on nightgowns, babies' and children's clothing and even craft projects, and its fascination for the embroiderer continues. Smocking can be as simple or ornate as you like. Two of the simple dresses in this section are from Simplicity Patterns. We have included these as good examples of practical smocking and have altered them slightly. These changes are clearly explained in our instructions.

Here are some examples of very intricate and clever smocking. The basic techniques are no different from the simplest smocking, the difference lies in the way in which the smocking has been embroidered with the delightful motifs. Note the clever use of buttons and frayed thread to give added texture and highlights.

Beautiful Blooms

Embroiderers everywhere are fascinated with flowers and floral shapes. Flowers are the single most frequently recurring motif in embroidery designs. But it's only natural that, as embroiderers love beauty in all forms, they will want to reflect nature's beauty in their stitches. Pretty cushion projects will show you how to bring beautiful blooms indoors with some delightfully simple stitching.

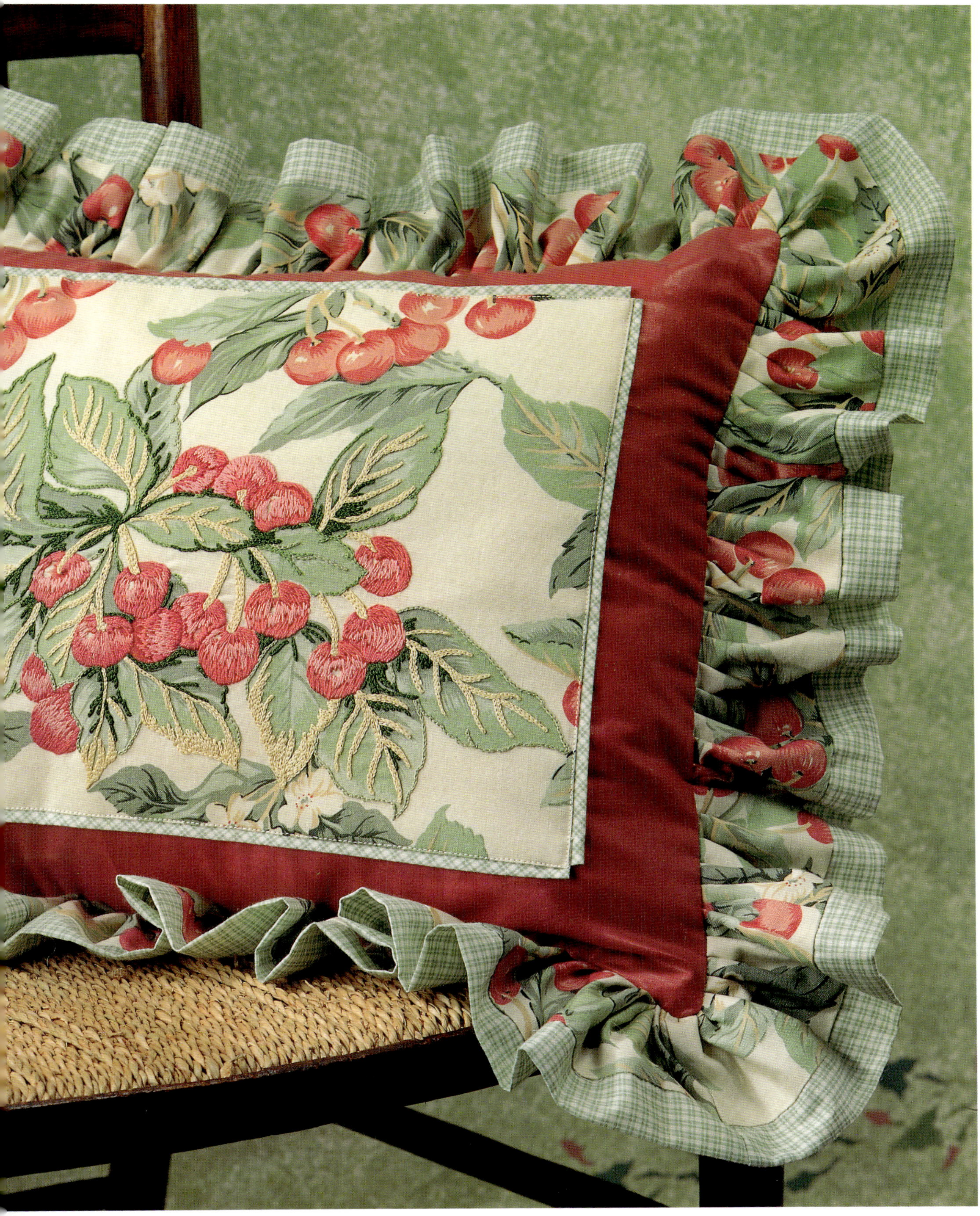

Re-embroidered Chintz Cushion

This cushion is shaped to suit the motif. We have used fabrics and colors to trim the ruffle that complement the chintz. Make your cushion in one fabric, big or small, or with a simple contrasting piping as you prefer. Whichever method you choose you are sure to have some very original floral embroideries.

STITCHES

The design of your fabric will suggest the best stitches to use in embroidering. Generally, the stems and fine vein lines are best worked in tiny Chain stitches – either in lines, or in curled 'snail shell' circles to fill in the larger areas. Work petals and other broad areas of color in Long and Short stitch. This gives you the opportunity to subtly vary the tones of color, by shading them across the area. French knots are ideal for small dots, or even for filling in the center of a flower, as the texture from grouped French knots is very attractive. Stem stitch and Satin stitch are also worth considering, and simple Blanket stitch is effective for outlining a flower.

All these stitches are outlined in the Stitch Guide at the front of the book. Work with an embroidery hoop to make your stitching easier and to prevent distortion of the fabric. Try to match closely the color of the embroidery floss to the color of your motif – the purpose of this type of embroidery is to embellish and add texture to the design, not to draw attention to any particular stitch.

MATERIALS

sufficient chintz fabric for the cushion front, border, cushion back and ruffle
sufficient contrasting fabric for the ruffle
sufficient 1" wide bias binding to go around the embroidered panel
6-strand embroidery floss in the colors of your choice
sewing thread
zipper
a cushion insert (purchased cushion insert or one made to measure)

METHOD

Make your cushion any size and shape that complements your fabric. Remember, your embroidered panel will be about 3 1/2" smaller than the finished cushion.

1 Re-embroider the center panel of your cushion in the stitches described above. When the embroidery is complete, turn under the outside edges of the panel and press.

2 Press open the 1" wide bias binding. Fold it in half lengthwise with right sides together. Press. Pin this bias binding under the edge of the embroidered panel so that the folded edge just protrudes. Overlap the two raw ends and then tuck them neatly out of sight under the embroidered panel. Baste.

3 Cut a piece of fabric the same shape as the embroidered panel

STITCHES USED

Chain Stitch for the stem and vein lines; Long and Short stitch for the petals and leaves but about 4" larger all around. Place the embroidered panel onto the center of the larger piece, taking care that the border is the same size all around. Stitch through all thicknesses around the embroidered panel.

4 Measure around the edge of the cushion front and cut two and a half times this amount of 4" wide fabric for the ruffle. Cut another identical length $4^{3}/4$" wide from a contrasting fabric. Join these two strips together along one long edge with right sides together. Join the short ends, with right sides together, to form a ring. Fold the circular strip in half with wrong sides together so that the raw edges are even and press. You should have a band of contrasting fabric at the outer edge of your ruffle ring. If your cushion is square, mark the ruffle into quarters. Gather the ruffle, starting and stopping your gathering thread at the quarter points. Pin the ruffle to the right side of the cushion front, placing the quarter points at the corners of the cushion front and having the raw edges even. Adjust the gathers to fit. If your cushion is oblong, mark half-way points along the long sides of the cushion front and mark the ruffle into two parts. Gather the ruffle, starting and stopping your gathering thread at the half-way points. Pin the ruffle around the right side of the cushion front, matching these two points and having the raw edges even. Adjust the gathers to fit.

5 Cut two back pieces, each one the same length as the front but half the width plus $1^{1}/4$". Join these pieces in a $1^{1}/4$" seam, leaving an opening in the center for the zipper. Insert zipper and leave it open.

6 Fold the ruffle towards the center of the embroidered panel. Place the cushion back over the ruffled cushion front with right sides together and raw edges matching. Stitch around the outside edge, following the stitching line for the ruffle and taking care not to catch the ruffle as you sew. Turn the cushion right side out through the zipper opening.

If a commercial cushion insert is not available in a size to suit your cushion, make a muslin bag the size of your cushion leaving an opening to insert polyester fiber stuffing or feathers. Once the cushion insert is filled, hand sew the opening closed.

THE SECRETS OF CHINTZ

Pretty flowered chintz, so evocative of charming country cottages and summer gardens, is widely regarded as being traditionally and thoroughly English. But chintz has a secret. It is true that chintz is traditional in England, but it is also traditional in Holland where it is called *sits* and in France where it is sometimes referred to as *indiennes* and that is where the secret lies. Yes, chintz originally came from India. The word 'chintz' is a corruption of a Hindi word *chint* or *chinta* meaning 'variegated' or 'spotted all over'. The chints, as they were originally called, were taken to Europe in the 1600s by the various East India companies, English, Dutch and French traders. They were a secondary import as the companies had gone to the East primarily to buy spices but found that Indian textiles, mainly cottons of all types, were part of the deal.

In England, the chints were tried only tentatively on the market, but soon took on and ultimately became the rage. For the first time people had lightweight cotton cloth that could be easily washed. Not only were the pretty patterns attractive but were printed in dyes that were fast. This was a miracle at the time. Europe had never known fast dyes before. Indian dyers had known how to dye cotton fast since ancient times and could produce more than one hundred colours and shades by their age-old methods. Another advantage was that the prices were low, so a large section of the population could afford them. The demand grew and by the mid-1600s the English company had imported well over a quarter of a million pieces. Everybody wanted chints!

There was the same craze in Holland where chintz was being used for clothing; and in France where *indiennes* or *toilet peintes* became the rage for fashionable clothing and for furnishing. The best Indian chintz was painted and resist dyed by a slow and tedious process called *kalamkari* (literally 'penwork'); but to speed up the output to meet the huge European demand block-printing, another old Indian method, was also used. Much admired among the painted clothes were the one-of-a-kind palampores (from *papangposh* meaning literally 'bedcover'). Many of these featured the 'Tree of Life' design, exotically embellished with luscious fruit, strange birds and animals in glowing colors. These became collectors' items and embroiderers loved to copy them. Embroidery was very popular in England at that time, with bedhangings and covers done in silks or in crewel wool work in flowing designs of English flowers and twining branches. Indian chintz, not dissimilar in design, was now being used.

Indian chintz and other cottons of all types continued to go to Europe for nearly two hundred years until Lancashire mastered cotton spinning and weaving. European textile printers, having found out the secrets of Indian cotton dyeing, were able to produce good copies of Indian chintz. Design differences began to develop in various countries, with English and French chintzes, for instance, gradually evolving into distinctive styles.

Chintz also traveled to faraway colonies such as Australia where large quantities of Indian cottons of all types, including chintz were imported.

In modern chintzes, Indian design influences can still be seen – look for stylized flowers, birds and paisley shapes that all reflect their Indian heritage.

Joyce Burnard is a journalist. She founded Ascraft fabrics, a firm which has specialised in importing Indian hand-loomed cotton into Australia. She has just completed a book which traces the fascinating connection of chintz and other Indian textiles with the West.

The chintzes on the opposite page were provided by Ascraft Fabric, Sydney

45

SILK FLORAL BOUDOIR CUSHION

This charming small cushion can be made from a remnant of lovely silk. Covered with small sprays of flowers, it is embroidered in simple, tiny stitches. Our cushion measures 25 cm x 25 cm but you could expand this size and simply repeat the embroidery motifs to fill the larger area. The lace is stitched on by hand.

STITCHES USED
Bullion stitch for the roses; Lazy Daisy stitch for the daisies; Satin stitch for petals and leaves; French knots for the dots; Stem stitch for the stems

MATERIALS
two pieces of silk for the back and front of the cushion
silk embroidery floss in the colors of your choice
sufficient $2^1/2$" wide lace
sewing thread
cushion insert to fit
embroidery needle

METHOD
See the Pull Out Transfer Sheet at the back of the book for the embroidery designs.

1 *For the embroidery:* Transfer the floral motifs onto one piece of silk, following the instructions on the Transfer Sheet. Embroider the flowers in the stitches indicated, following the Stitch Guide at the front of the book.

2 *For the sewing:* When you have finished embroidering, place the cushion front and back right sides together and raw edges even. Stitch around the edge, leaving an opening for turning. Turn cushion right side out. Place the cushion insert inside and close the opening by hand.

3 *To finish off:* Sew the lace around the cushion by aligning the straight edge of the lace with the cushion seam and taking small stitches every $1/4$" along the cushion edge, pushing the lace into folds between the stitches. Overlap and neaten the ends of the lace when the stitching is complete.

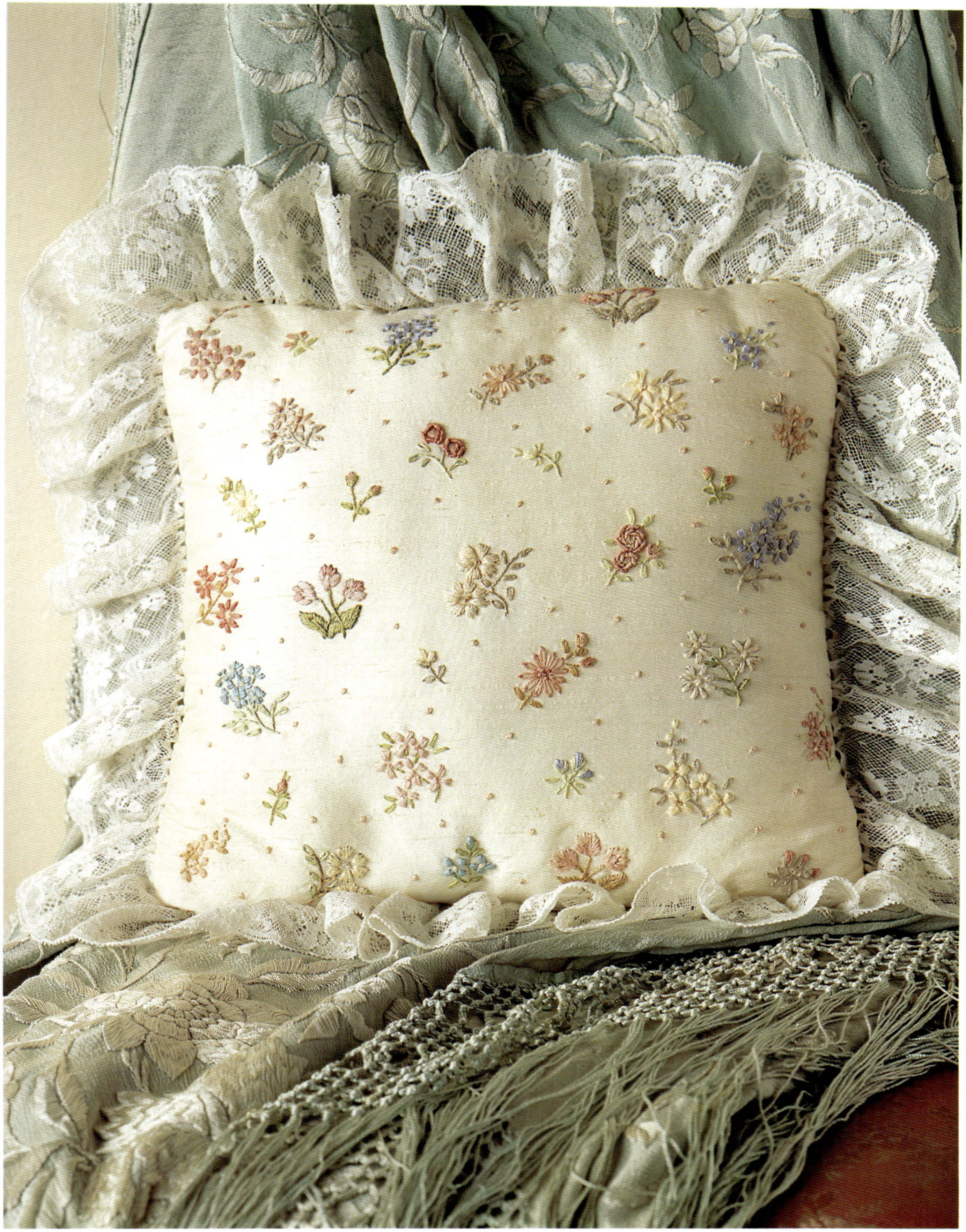

CROSS-STITCH CUSHION

To make this pretty cushion match the colours of your embroidery to a favourite fine cotton print – perhaps to an existing fabric in your home. There is wonderful scope here for a truly unique approach to embroidery.

MATERIALS

14½" square of white hardanger fabric with 22-threads-to-1"
6-strand embroidery floss in your chosen colors. We used the DMC colors as indicated on the graph
2⅓ yds cotton cording for piping
2⅓ yds 1" wide bias binding
2½ yds of 36" wide fine cotton
20" cushion insert
sewing thread
16" zipper
embroidery needle

METHOD

1 *For cutting out:* From the cotton fabric cut four strips each 5" x 20" for the cushion border; cut 5½ yds of 8" wide strips for the ruffle (join pieces if necessary to achieve the desired length) and two pieces 20" x 11¼" for the cushion back.

2 *For the embroidery:* Working with an embroidery hoop, embroider the hardanger panel following the chart and stitch key. Each stitch should be worked over 2 threads. On each side, draw out three threads 2½" from the edge and Hemstitch along the row of holes, following the Stitch Guide at the front of the book.

3 *For the border:* Cut the ends of the border strips at 45° angles and join them into an open square, stopping the stitching ⅜" from the inner edge of each corner. Press under ⅜" on the inner edge of the border. Pin and baste this border evenly around the edge of the embroidered panel. Stitch along the pressed edge through all thicknesses.

4 *For the piping:* Unfold the bias binding and press it flat. Fold it in half lengthwise. Insert cotton cording into the fold and stitch it in place, using the zipper foot of your sewing machine. Baste this piping around the edge of the right side of the cushion front, clipping at the corners for ease.

5 *For the ruffle:* Join the ruffle strips into a ring. Press it in half with wrong sides together and raw edges even. Divide and mark the ruffle into quarters with pins. Gather along the raw edge, starting and finishing at the quarter points. Pin the ruffle to the right side of the cushion front, with raw edges even, matching quarter

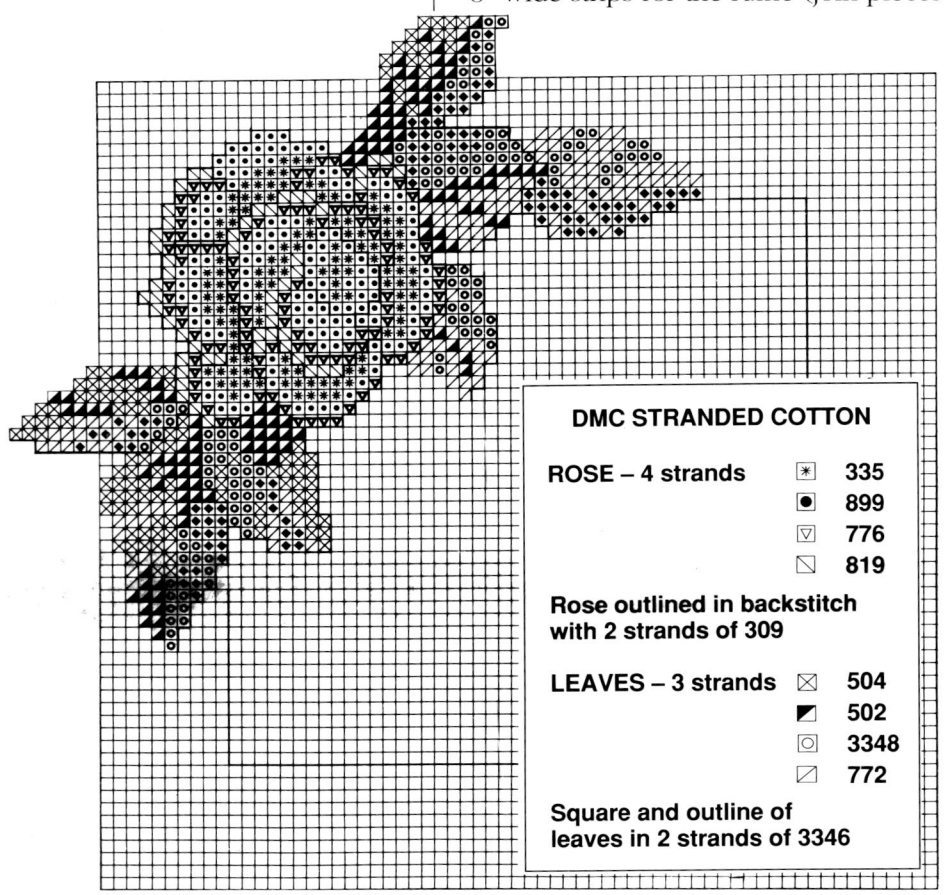

DMC STRANDED COTTON

ROSE – 4 strands
- ✳ 335
- ● 899
- ▽ 776
- ◻ 819

Rose outlined in backstitch with 2 strands of 309

LEAVES – 3 strands
- ⊠ 504
- ◤ 502
- ⊙ 3348
- ⊠ 772

Square and outline of leaves in 2 strands of 3346

points to corners. Adjust the gathers to fit. Stitch the ruffle in place, taking care not to stitch through the piping cord.

6 *For the cushion back:* Stitch the back sections together along the 20" edge, using a 1¼" seam allowance, and leaving a 16" opening for the zipper at the center of the seam. Press the seam open and insert the zipper. Leave the zipper open.

7 *To assemble the cushion:* Fold the ruffle toward the center of the embroidered panel. Place back and front right sides together and raw edges even. Stitch around the edge following the previous stitching. Turn the cushion right side out through the zipper opening.

49

Embroider a Stencil

Hand appliqué has always looked exquisite because it is so detailed and intricate. This can be an obstacle, preventing beginners taking up this pleasing embroidery. Here is the answer! This lovely cloth has been stenciled and re-embroidered to give the same textured effect.

51

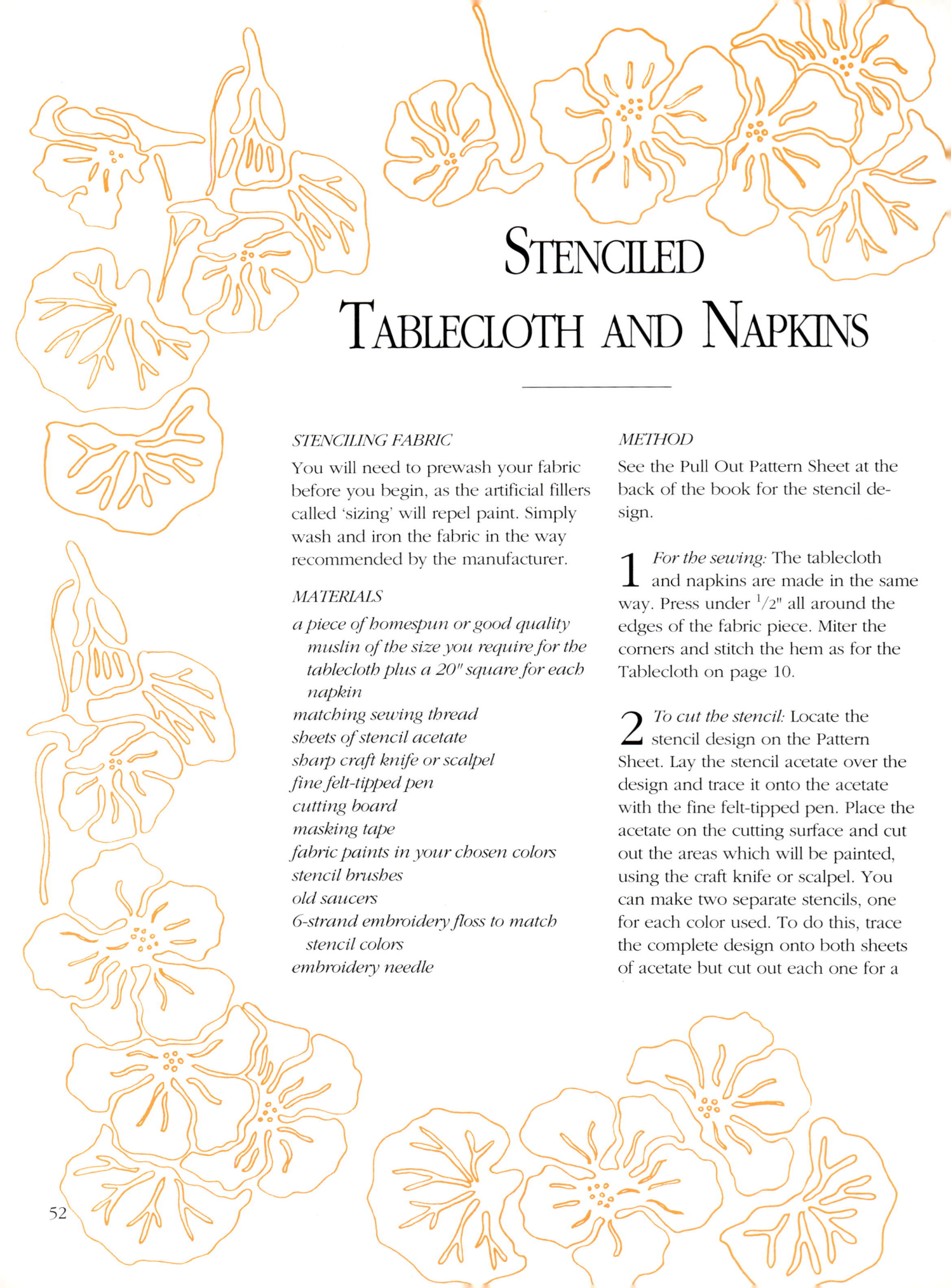

Stenciled Tablecloth and Napkins

STENCILING FABRIC

You will need to prewash your fabric before you begin, as the artificial fillers called 'sizing' will repel paint. Simply wash and iron the fabric in the way recommended by the manufacturer.

MATERIALS

a piece of homespun or good quality muslin of the size you require for the tablecloth plus a 20" square for each napkin
matching sewing thread
sheets of stencil acetate
sharp craft knife or scalpel
fine felt-tipped pen
cutting board
masking tape
fabric paints in your chosen colors
stencil brushes
old saucers
6-strand embroidery floss to match stencil colors
embroidery needle

METHOD

See the Pull Out Pattern Sheet at the back of the book for the stencil design.

1 *For the sewing:* The tablecloth and napkins are made in the same way. Press under $1/2$" all around the edges of the fabric piece. Miter the corners and stitch the hem as for the Tablecloth on page 10.

2 *To cut the stencil:* Locate the stencil design on the Pattern Sheet. Lay the stencil acetate over the design and trace it onto the acetate with the fine felt-tipped pen. Place the acetate on the cutting surface and cut out the areas which will be painted, using the craft knife or scalpel. You can make two separate stencils, one for each color used. To do this, trace the complete design onto both sheets of acetate but cut out each one for a single color only. The rest of the traced design will help you position the stencil.

3 *For painting the stencil:* Position the motifs in the corners of your fabric. Note that the napkins are stenciled in one corner only and the border goes around all four sides. Hold the stencil in place with small strips of masking tape. If you are using a single stencil for both colors, it is helpful to cover adjoining areas of the other color with masking tape. Pour a small quantity of paint into a saucer and spread it out. Stencils require very little paint compared to other painting techniques. Using a dry brush and a dabbing, rather than a stroking, movement paint in the design, working from the edges towards the center of an area. Wipe off any excess paint. Too much paint on the brush or even a wet brush will cause the paint to seep under the edges of the stencil and give an indistinct outline. Allow the paint to dry between colors to avoid running. Additional highlights can be painted over the top of the stenciled design to give depth and texture to the shapes, for example we painted over yellow with a deeper orange. Keep your stencil clean – wash it between uses, especially if you are using one stencil for both colors.

4 *To stencil the border:* Work out your color and pattern distribution before you begin painting. Stencil all around first with one color, allow it to dry then replace the stencil in the spaces you have left and fill in the second color. Try moving the stencil for different angles of flowers and leaves, and taking elements out of the design and repositioning them. The stenciled border should link up with the bunch of flowers on both sides. Set the paints according to the manufacturer's directions.

5 *For the embroidery:* Stitch around the leaves and flowers using Blanket stitch as shown in the Stitch Guide at the front of the book. Choose colors to match the colors of the paints. Remember you want this stitching to be visible so don't make the individual stitches too small. Be sure to follow the edges of the flowers and leaves accurately.

Charming Cross-stitch

Of all the embroidery stitches, Cross-stitch is the most popular. Use it on a sampler, a tapestry or a delicately embroidered linen handkerchief and matching jewelry cushion.

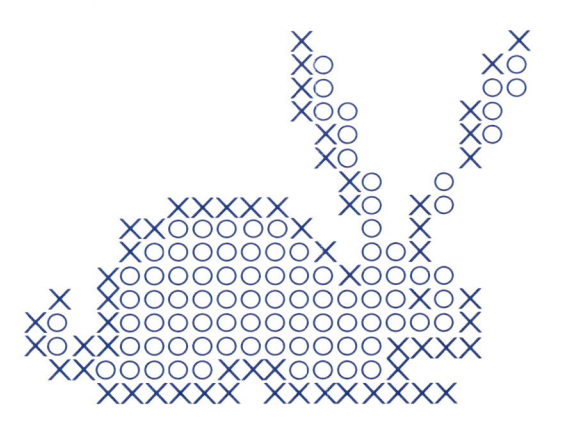

55

Monogrammed Handkerchief

The perfect gifts to embroider for someone special, this dainty handkerchief and jewelry cushion are sure to be treasured for a long time. You can make your own handkerchief or buy one to embroider.

MATERIALS

a square of handkerchief linen
wide single edged lace to trim the edge
4" square of waste canvas (14-threads-to-the-inch)
6-strand embroidery floss in the colors of your choice
embroidery needle

METHOD

See the Pull Out Pattern Sheet at the back of the book for the Cross-stitch alphabet graph.

1 *For the lace:* Draw threads from each edge of the linen square and trim to make certain all the edges are perfectly straight. Press in 1/4" all around the square. Stitch the lace under the pressed edge, mitering or gathering it at the corners.

2 *For the embroidery:* Baste the edges of a piece of waste canvas, large enough to accommodate your letter, over one corner of the handkerchief. Locate the letter you require on the Pattern Sheet and embroider it over the waste canvas, through the linen as well, using two strands of embroidery floss. When the embroidery is complete, carefully draw out the canvas, thread by thread, leaving the Cross-stitch motif on the linen.

Jewelry Cushion

MATERIALS

two pieces of linen each 5 1/4" x 4"
two strips of linen each 4" x 2"
two strips of linen each 5 1/4" x 2"
4" square of waste canvas (14-threads-to-the-inch)
6-strand embroidery floss in the colors of your choice
1 1/2 yds colored twisted cord
small quantity of polyester fiber for stuffing
iron-on interfacing
sewing thread
embroidery needle

METHOD

See the Pull Out Pattern Sheet at the back of the book for the Cross-stitch alphabet graph. 3/8" seams allowed all around each pattern piece.

1 *For the embroidery:* Find the center of one square of linen by folding it in half lengthwise and crosswise. The intersection of the folds is the center point. Baste the edges of a piece of waste canvas, large enough to accommodate your letter, over this center point. Locate the letter you require on the Pattern Sheet and embroider it over the waste canvas, through the linen as well, using two strands of embroidery thread. When the embroidery is complete, carefully draw out the canvas thread by thread, leaving the Cross-stitch motif on the linen.

2 *For the sewing:* Interface all pieces of linen. Pin the short ends of all the strips together to form an open box. Check that it fits around the edge of the embroidered linen. Adjust the

STITCHES USED
Cross-stitch for all motifs

Above: Jewelry Cushion
Right: Monogrammed Handkerchief

length if necessary. Pin the strip around the edge of the embroidered linen, with raw edges even, right sides together and seams matching to the corners. Stitch. Pin the remaining piece of linen to the remaining edge of the strip with right sides together, raw edges even and seams matching to the corners again. Stitch, leaving an opening for turning. Turn the cushion right side out, pushing the corners out neatly. Stuff the cushion firmly and close the opening by hand. Hand sew the twisted cord around the edges of the cushion; on the top, shape it into three small loops at each corner, resembling a clover leaf. Start and finish at a corner, tucking the ends of the cord out of sight behind a loop at the end.

THE STORY OF SAMPLERS

Samplers were, just as their name implies, a piece of fabric stitched to demonstrate various sewing techniques that allowed the stitchers to display their talents. For a long time, samplers actually functioned as job applications, being presented to a prospective employer to show off the talents of the seamstress. Up until quite recently, girls who were schooled in the traditional sewing crafts would make a darning sampler, a Cross-stitch sampler and perhaps a fancy embroidery sampler.

Often samplers were totally spontaneous, with the design taking shape as the stitcher worked her way through the project. These samplers could show simple rows of stitches, tucks, gathers, collections of a particular motif – perhaps animals, flowers or houses, or they could even depict the family tree, dates of birth and the occupations and interests of the family members. If these talented women were sentimental enough to keep their works of art, chances are they are beautifully framed and displayed in their homes as a permanent reminder of their skills.

Samplers still have the element of variety, but perhaps not so much as yesterday. Today they show names and dates, wise sayings, alphabets or special motifs to commemorate a great occasion. Samplers still demand the same skills and, of course, the more accurate the work the better the finished product looks. Cross-stitch has become the modern day sampler stitch, with endless examples available in kits, or as counted Cross-stitch in embroidery books. It's important to have your sampler properly framed and preserved. Cast your eye over our photographs of samplers past and present, and perhaps you'll be inspired to embark on your own sentimental journey.

Samplers from Simply Stitches

On this page and on the opposite page are some delightful examples of embroidered samplers, showing the almost limitless variety that you can achieve with simple Cross stitch. You can choose something as simple as the alphabet (below) or one as intricate as the Bird in Hand sampler at the bottom of the page. Ideally, the motifs should reflect some aspect of your life and interests or contain some message that you wish to convey. In the past, these messages were often religious ones, such as the Lord's prayer or the story of Noah's ark (opposite page).

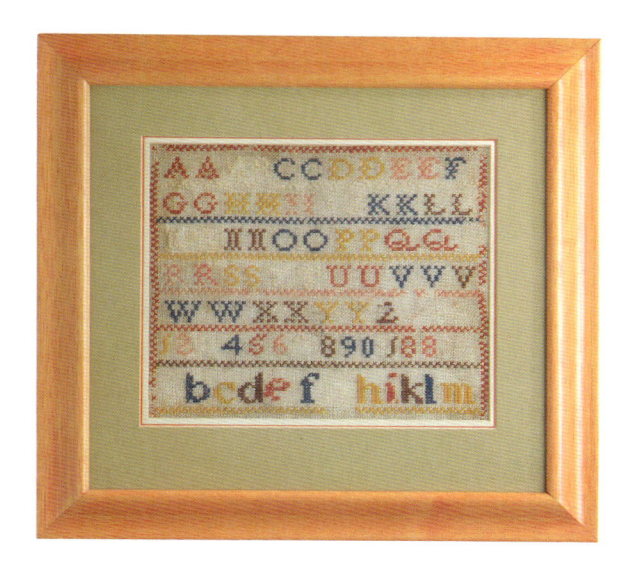

FESTIVE SAMPLER

This charming mix of a monogram and a floral spray gives a fresh, contemporary feel to an otherwise traditional sampler motif. Alternatively, you can take letters from the alphabet and spell out the name of someone special, keeping the floral border and sprays. This would give the sampler a horizontal shape, rather than the vertical shape it is now.

MATERIALS
a piece of Zweigart Lugana 18" x 23" (25-threads-to-the-inch)
6-strand embroidery floss in the following DMC colors: 3350; 963; 899; 761; 3364; 3362; 472; 800; 793
tapestry needle

METHOD
See the Pull Out Pattern Sheet at the back of the book for the Cross-stitch alphabet chart and color key.

1. *To find the center:* Mark the center of your fabric vertically and horizontally with a line of basting. Where these lines intersect is the middle of your fabric. Draw a pencil line connecting the arrows on each side of the chart. This point is the center of the chart and should correspond with the center of the fabric. Start counting from this point.

2. *For the embroidery:* Each symbol on the chart represents one Cross-stitch; the different symbols indicate the colors to be used. Embroider, using two strands of floss and Cross-stitch, following the Stitch Guide at the front of the book. Each stitch should be worked over two fabric threads. Do not tie knots but begin and end a strand by running the needle through the back of a few stitches at the back of the work. Using a tapestry roller frame or a large embroidery hoop will make the work easier.

3. *For the framing:* On completion of the embroidery, it is important to have your sampler framed by someone specializing in this type of work.

STITCHES USED
Cross-stitch for all the motifs

This Festive Cross Stitch Sampler is from DMC Needlecraft Pty Ltd and is worked in DMC threads.

61

CORNELLI WOOL EMBROIDERY

This is a very simple yet effective trim for any woolen garment – and it can be used on lighter fabrics too. Cornelli work is the effect of one long continuous line of stitching, forming a pattern of loops and curves.

MATERIALS
a purchased wool pullover or cardigan
suitable yarn for working the stitches
tapestry needle

METHOD

1 *For the design:* Mark out your design area with basting. If you are not confident enough to make the design as you go, mark out your Cornelli lines with a soft lead pencil or chalk. You will find it becomes much easier with a little practice. The design given here is a guide – adjust it to suit your design area.

2 *For the embroidery:* The basic stitch used in the embroidery is Chain stitch, though any 'straight' stitch can be effective. We chose Chain stitch as it is fairly bulky and results come quickly. Two different weights of yarn were used – one a textured chenille knitting yarn and another knitting yarn made from smooth glossy silk. Stitch two parallel lines in a random wavy line that keeps turning back on itself until the basted area is covered.

3 *To finish off:* Consider changing the buttons on your cardigan to complement the embroidery. Make the shape of your embroidery suit your garment. For a small area such as a shoulder or the point at center front, bring the stitching into a point where you can later attach a tassel made from yarn to complete the effect!

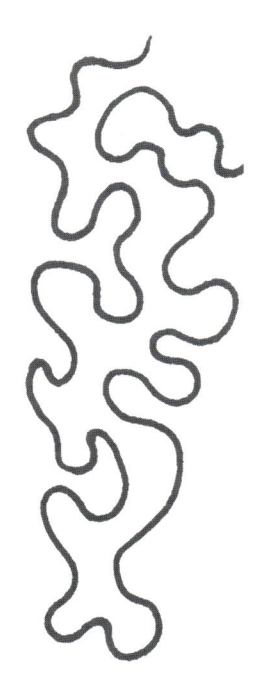

STITCHES USED
Chain stitch

Left: See how Cornelli work is simply the effect of two wiggly lines of chain stitch working together to form the pattern

63

Here are some additional embroidery designs for you to use. You can embroider them using many of the stitches found in the Stitch Guide at the front of the book.

ACKNOWLEDGEMENTS

The publishers would like to thank the following people who assisted with production of this book: David Jones own brand for the woollen jumpers; Liberty for the fabric for the smocked dresses; DMC for embroidery supplies; Offray for ribbons; Simplicity Patterns Australia for the dress patterns; Antiques loaned by Robyn Macintosh, Michelle Gleason and Barbara Shorter.

How To Use The Transfer Sheet

- Preheat iron. Set to recommended temperature for each fabric.
- Do not use steam.
- Cut out chosen design and position it onto fabric, INK SIDE DOWN.
- Place the iron directly on the transfer pattern – press, lift and look (check how dark the design looks by carefully lifting one corner while holding the rest of the design in place). Do not slide the iron the same way you do when you are ironing! THE DESIGN COULD SMEAR.
- After the entire design is transferred, let it cool a little before removing the pattern.
- Transfers can be used more than once, but they get lighter each time. To extend the life, iron-on transfer pencils are available at fabric and craft stores. Simply trace over pattern lines with special pencil and transfer.
- The lines on the transfers will fade with each use. Since we have used the transfer lines as details in some of our designs, we suggest the use of a permanent fabric outline pen to fill them in or darken them. These pens are available at craft and fabric stores.